TIPPED

The life-changing guide to financial freedom for waitresses, bartenders, strippers, and all other service industry professionals

Barbara Sloan

Copyright © 2022 by Barbara Sloan

All rights reserved. No part of this publication may be reproduced, distributed, or transmitted in any form or by any means, including photocopying, recording, or other electronic or mechanical methods, without the prior written permission of the publisher, except in the case of brief quotations embodied in critical reviews and certain other noncommercial uses permitted by copyright law. For permission requests, write to the publisher, addressed "Attention: Permissions Coordinator," at Barbara@TippedFinance.com.

ISBN 979-8-9856481-0-2 (Paperback)
ISBN 979-8-9856481-2-6 (Hardcover)
ISBN 979-8-9856481-1-9 (ebook)

Library of Congress Control Number: 2022915441

Front cover design by Vanessa Mendozzi
Edited and interior designed by Danielle Anderson at Ink Worthy Books

Printed by Barbara Sloan in the United States of America.

First printing edition 2022.
www.TippedFinance.com

FOR EDUCATIONAL AND INFORMATIONAL PURPOSES ONLY.
NOT LEGAL OR FINANCIAL ADVICE.

The information provided in this book is for educational and informational purposes only and solely as a self-help tool for your own use. All content reflects the author's opinion at a given time and can change as time progresses. All information should be taken as an opinion and should not be misconstrued for professional or legal advice. The contents of this book are informational in nature and are not legal or tax advice, and the author and publisher are not engaged in the provision of legal, tax, or any other advice.

I am not an attorney, accountant, or financial advisor, nor am I holding myself out to be. I am a former bartender, and while bartenders give great advice, the information contained in this book is not intended to be a substitute for legal or financial advice that can be provided by your own attorney, accountant, and/or financial advisor. Although care has been taken in preparing the information provided to you, I cannot be held responsible for any errors or omissions, and I accept no liability whatsoever for any loss or damage you may incur. Investing always involves risk. Always seek financial and/or legal counsel relating to your specific circumstances as needed for any and all questions and concerns you now have or may have in the future.

This book is dedicated to...

All the SIPs who are ready to take control of the things they can. Your passion for the art of service is a gift to the world. If this is your calling or craft, lean in.

Casey. Your respect and love have given me the space and support always to be my truest self, and for that I am forever grateful.

Table of Contents

Foreword iii

Introduction vii

Chapter One 1
Please Wait to Be Seated: *How our industry has excluded us from traditional wealth building paths*

Chapter Two 17
Front of House, But Back of Mind: *How our environment might be shaping our financial lives*

Chapter Three 27
You're a Hustler; Hustle Responsibly: *Your competitive advantages and how to make more money*

Chapter Four 43
Budget Like No One is Watching (Because No One is Watching): *Why you need a budget, how to make one, and how to ride it like the bitch it is*

Chapter Five 67
Pay Your Sexy Self First: *How to reset your financial priorities to serve you first*

Chapter Six 75
In Case of Fire (or Getting Fired), Break Glass: *How this one account will change your entire life*

Chapter Seven 89
Who Ordered the Credit Topped With Debt? *Why credit and debt aren't THAT important to your financial health and how to get them to take a backseat*

Chapter Eight 103
Keep Your Drinks Close and Your Investments Closer: *Your one-stop shop to understanding what the hell investing even is and how you can get started*

Chapter Nine 125
Cover Your Ass (When You Aren't Twerking): *How to protect what you are growing with insurance and estate planning*

Chapter Ten 135
Money on Your Mind(set): *Why your mindset matters more than the math*

Last Call 151

About the Author 155

Appendix 1 157
Road Map for Financial Freedom

Appendix 2 158
Additional Concepts for Financial Freedom

Appendix 3 160
Be Your Own Sharon

Appendix 4 162
Compound Calculator and Examples

Appendix 5 163
Monthly Budget Tracker

Appendix 6 164
Net Worth Tracker

Foreword

If you're a service industry provider (SIP)—whether you're a bartender, server, barback, usher, hairstylist, facialist, nail salon worker, concierge, valet, stripper, or anyone else whose income is highly dependent on tips—then I immediately know three things about your financial life:

1. You've been underserved by traditional financial media. The cacophony of books, magazines, blogs, podcasts, YouTube videos, and TikToks that attempt to teach people how to manage and grow their money are mostly aimed at the office-dwelling, salaried nine-to-five crowd.
2. You may be scraping by, or you may be making six figures, depending on your industry, experience, location, position, and hours. Your income may fluctuate within a wide range. However, regardless of how much you make, you're unlikely to be receiving the types of benefits salaried office workers in the U.S. typically enjoy, such as retirement packages, paid time off, and employer-sponsored health insurance.

3. Your job is likely to be physically demanding, which means that even if you plan on being an industry lifer, you need to prepare for the possibility that aches, pains and injuries may force you into an earlier retirement than you'd hoped for.

The first point highlights a massive shortcoming in the popular financial press. The second and third points emphasize why this is a critical problem for service professionals.

This book is part of the solution that addresses all three points.

Author Barbara Sloan, who spent two decades in the service industry as a server, bartender, and stripper, understands exactly what industry life is like.

She's lived in her car; she's worked overnight shifts. She speaks to you as an insider. She happens to be an insider who figured out the financial puzzle, partly from her time in the service industry, partly from her time on Wall Street, partly from her time running a small business, but largely through grit, determination, and by absorbing thousands of hours of financial media. Along the way, she developed critical judgment (after all, there's a lot of crap advice out there mixed in with the good advice, and it takes a certain skill set to sniff out the difference), and she learned the core principles of how to handle money.

Now, in *Tipped*, she distills her decades of knowledge into one book which you're holding in your hands (or reading on your screen).

Before you start reading, here are a few things you should know:

1. Don't assume this book is limited to number crunching. Yes, the words "money management" might conjure images of boring budgets and spreadsheets, but mastering your money starts with mindset and psychology. This book addresses these important elements throughout. Barbara lists the emotional and financial hazards of the job (shitty customers, too many hangovers, etc.) and offers tactics on how to cope. She discusses budgetary

boundary setting and discretion. She talks about how to handle shame, guilt, and burnout. She describes why she thought the concept of mindset sounded "woo-woo" and how she overcame this limiting belief to reach financial success.
2. You'll learn how to make a budget while on a fluctuating income, build an emergency fund, track your net worth, and invest for the long-term. But equally as important, you'll learn how to cope with what comes up during this process. The emotions you may feel as you face your finances can run high; Barbara is here to normalize the process and walk you through it like a wise older sister who's been in your shoes and knows what's up.
3. The Intimidating "I's"—investing and insurance—are not as complicated as you think. In fact, you can use a bartending metaphor to simplify and help you understand how the system works. Once you're armed with this knowledge, you'll never need to overpay some stuffy suit-and-tie to handle it for you. More importantly, you'll be empowered to make decisions for yourself about your own hard-earned tips.

Taking control of your tipped income—and growing your money without having to pick up extra shifts—is one of the most empowering moves you can make. This book is the start of that journey.

—Paula Pant
Host, *Afford Anything* Podcast

Introduction

    I was 16 years old, standing in a parking lot under a flood lamp and stripping down—one by one—the 33 pink thongs I wish I had thought to put on in order of sizing. Around me there were a few other girls looking as if they too knew the pain of having all that fabric jammed way too far up their asses. There was also a large group of mall-goers, workers, and two disc jockeys who were blaring Pink's "Most Girls" from their seats at the sliding side door of the radio station's van. They cheered me on as the crowd counted each pair of panties I dropped (all but the last, of course).

    See, I was entering a radio station contest to win tickets to a Pink concert, and the winner would be the girl who showed up to the parking lot location wearing the highest number of pink thongs. I was working one of my after-school jobs at the JC Penney in the mall—it was just my luck the contest was going to be held in the mall parking lot right as my shift ended. Upon hearing the details for the contest, I quickly ran to the discount underwear bin and pulled out all the pink thongs I could find that were less than $2. I showed up waddling, confident in my win, and was surprised to find that in order to be officially entered into the contest, we had to do a showcase of taking them off one by one, so they could count them. A few weeks after winning those front row tickets, I was invited to a party by the mall security staff and asked to perform the same routine for $300, plus tips. This was my entry into stripping, service work, and the tipped life.

Over fifteen years later and after a pole dancing injury went from bad to worse (you can only whip your hair to "Walk This Way" so many times a week with a neck and shoulder injury), I went in search of a desk job with health insurance. I found myself in an accounting department, pretending to know how to do financial analysis on Wall Street, working for a company that was part trading floor and part sales organization for large cash advances, also known as loan sharking. This was a huge education for me, not only on the stock market, but also on the predatory nature of financial service companies (more on that later). I saw how they took advantage of uneducated people, people in debt, small business owners, and even other traders who worked alongside them. After seeing a third trader shipped off to rehab, I left to work for a general contractor who did renovations for high-net-worth clients.

There, I had the opportunity to work directly with wealthy individuals on their renovation budgets. It was a pivotal moment for me. It helped me understand how wealthy individuals think about money and their investments. The contracting company was small; I was their fifth employee. It was growing quickly, and I was afforded the opportunity to grow with it. One of my tasks was setting up a human resources (HR) department and benefits package. Through this process, I gained firsthand knowledge of how 401(k)s, health insurance, direct deposit, pre-tax contributions, and PTO complimented and supported the financial lives of each of the employees. Though I had known these benefits were common in most industries, it wasn't until I fully understood and was benefiting from them that I began to realize all the ways tipped employees miss out on traditional wealth building opportunities, not to mention how starkly SIPs lack even the most basic of financial safety nets.

INTRODUCTION

Then, in 2016, the political landscape was a mess. My anxiety was at an all-time high, and I just couldn't stomach the news cycle any longer. I decided to do a media blackout for a year. No news, no streaming, no scrolling on social media. With all this newfound time on my hands, lengthened considerably by long hours of commuting, I decided to dive deep into the world of personal finance. I figured I could use the time to make some positive changes in my life. I also thought that if I became really good with managing my money, it would put me in a position to be able to donate more money to charities with values I held near to my heart. I may not have been a congressperson, but I figured at least if I could learn more about money, I could still make a financial impact. Unbeknownst to me, that choice would single-handedly change my life; though I didn't know it at the time, it was also the beginning of this book.

You see, the further I went down the rabbit hole, the more I could see that this information was transformative, but it was clear that my SIP friends and coworkers couldn't relate to the topic of personal finance, at least in the way it was being packaged by industry experts at that time. No one was talking directly to SIPs—I knew I needed to do something to change that, and this is where you come in. You are here because you want to make some changes. Maybe you've realized that getting by from shift to shift hasn't translated into the goals you'd hoped for. You may be feeling shame about mistakes in your past, about the milestones you haven't achieved; you may feel you are behind, or maybe you just have a deep knowing that something is missing. Whatever it is that brought you here, it's because you want more, and more is what you will get.

There are a lot of jobs within the service industry: server, bartender, stripper, coat checker, valet, cocktail waiter, barista, go-go dancer, taxi driver, cater waiter, beer girl, hairstylist, escort, Coyote, etc. Throughout the book I refer to all people in the service industry as SIPs (service industry professionals). SIP employment can look different from person to person, place to place, and region to region, but what all SIPs share is that tips are a large part of their financial compensation. SIPs get tips! As a SIP, the three positions I held the longest were server, bartender, and stripper. In this book, I speak mostly from my experience within those positions, all set inside clubs, bars, and restaurants. Even if that isn't your direct experience as a SIP, the principles are still the same and applicable for people earning tips and living on a fluctuating income.

Regardless of whether you plan to be in the service industry only for a short time, plan on being a lifer, or if you are just going with the flow and keeping your options open, the concepts we discuss will serve (pun intended) you wherever you are. The systems you set up and the knowledge you gain will work in any fluctuating life and will help smooth out the ride. You plan on dealing with money for the rest of your life, so now is the best time to get very, *very* good with it. You would never leave money on the bar, so you will learn how not to do that in life.

If you've spent even a few months in the industry, you've likely experienced frustrations surrounding your work: slow shifts, unfair cuts, selfish coworkers, demanding managers, or getting stiffed—these are only some of the day-to-day problems. You've also likely had some satisfying times as well: busy shifts when you are in the flow, the perfect early cut, quality time with awesome coworkers, the perfect schedule, fun guests, and generous tippers—these are the joys. In between the problems and the joys, it's easy to lose sight of—or never really catch a glimpse of—the future or the road ahead. Many of you may not even realize you're operating without a map or a larger plan. As someone who spent two decades in the service industry (and also occasionally left the service industry), I understand that many people reading this don't have a plan (I certainly didn't) or may have a plan to leave the industry. Whether you have a plan to leave, don't have any plan, or enjoy the life you lead, this book will help you lay a financial foundation to support you.

The world and our industry can set us up for failure, and as a result, many of us have failed at times (I have so many financial failures), but it's in those moments that we pick ourselves up (again and again) and look for new ways to grow and improve to a point where real success is found. By reading this book, you are taking a big step toward a better understanding of the money in your world and what your financial options really are. Congratulate yourself and feel proud. Wherever you are on your journey, it is extremely important to recognize and celebrate the small steps you are taking toward progress. You are here now, trying, learning, and growing—and that means everything. Perhaps you will even allow yourself to dream of reaching a place where you are "financially free."

But what does that even mean, "financial freedom"? What is it, and why would we want to strive for it? Financial freedom, financial literacy, financial wholeness, financial independence. These terms are frequently thrown out in the world of personal finance, often when discussing milestones, strategies, or philosophies. It's okay if you aren't familiar with any or all of these terms. I wasn't, either, until I started studying personal finance. In fact, when I started in the industry, I thought financial freedom simply meant you were rich. Now, I interpret financial freedom[1] to mean two things:

1. You are in <u>control</u> of your own finances.
2. You are in <u>control</u> of your choices.

While on my own journey to financial freedom, I thought I was learning mostly about finances, but what I was really learning about was control.

As SIPs, we often think we don't have a lot of control. We can't always control our schedule or our guests, and we certainly can't control our tips. In this book, we explore all the areas where we do have control and how we can grow that control over time. First, we'll talk about why things are different for SIPs and why it is so much harder for you to get access to this information. Second, we will explore how to put together a spending plan (aka budget) while working with a fluctuating income. Third, we will review some good guidelines and rules of thumb to follow when spending. Fourth, I will walk you

---

[1] You can find an overview of what financial freedom is, along with a brief road map to financial freedom, in Appendix 1.

through how to get started on your own financial freedom path and to systemize your investing, as well as all your options, in an easy-to-understand way. Finally, I will outline the ways you can protect yourself and what you are growing.

If all these things sound good, and you are thinking, *Yes! Let's get down to it*, that's phenomenal! First, a quick disclaimer: If you came here for a certified financial professional to give you professional financial advice, then I'll save you time and tell you I am not that, and I don't do that. I have zero paper credentials—zip, zilch, nada. I'm also not someone who can properly address or solve the inequalities in our world or industry. However, maybe I've got something even better.

As humans, we most connect to—and learn from—stories, ones that closely resemble our own experiences. As a fellow SIP, what I do have is stories and tons of experiences in the service industry. I also have experience in the world of personal finance, in accounting and finance, and on my own journey to gaining financial freedom. Because I now have the vantage point to see what is possible, I want everyone in the service industry to find financial freedom. That being said, I've decided to put all I've learned, as well as how it can be applied to a SIP life, into a book I wish had been available at any point on my journey, especially at the beginning of my decades-long career in the service industry.

During the hundreds of hours I spent listening to finance podcasts and reading intro to personal finance and investing guides, I kept coming across the same advice being doled out, time after time, for corporate nine-to-fivers. Listeners or readers would write in, guests would come on, the same information would be recycled, and the same jargon would be used over and over. I heard advice on how millennials should cut out their daily lattes and questions such as how to ask for a raise or how to ask your parents for help with your six-figure student loans.

At no point did I see myself in any of the readers' or listeners' questions, and at no point did the guests offer actionable advice for someone like me, someone who spent the majority of her career in the service industry. Personal finance is personal,

INTRODUCTION

but in a space as large as this one, why wasn't I seeing or hearing anyone like me?

Unlike the financial advisors, coaches, and bloggers giving out this advice, I was afforded a rare glimpse into the reality of working within the service and hospitality industry for a long period of time. I could see then, as well as now, that the service industry has been largely ignored by the world of personal finance, and it has been preyed upon by the predatory side of the financial services industry. When I eventually stepped away from the tipped life, I saw the other side through my work growing small businesses and budgeting for high-net-worth clients, and I learned how people can use small sets of systems and mental frameworks to create financial abundance.

Over the years, I have figured out ways to make these classic concepts and advice work for those in the service industry. I would like the millions of service industry professionals who have never been offered a road map to be able to create one alongside me. I can show you that you can achieve your dreams in the careers you have chosen, and this includes those who may just consider the service industry to be a temporary career. I want you to feel supported and to know your money is real money, your careers are real careers, and that in going on this journey with me, working the steps, and creating a financial plan, you will be on the path to a future filled with more options and brighter choices.

By the time you finish this book, you will have a plan for how to create and improve your financial life, and you will have advice specifically for navigating the service industry while growing your wealth. You will have a better understanding of how to get your position and career to align with your money goals and how to avoid industry pitfalls. With knowledge comes confidence, and with confidence comes more money. I encourage you to find what works for you and leave what doesn't.

To all the waitresses, bartenders, dancers, sex workers, valet attendants, hairstylists, bouncers, barbacks, go-go dancers, coat checkers, ushers, door people, concierges, strippers, and anyone else who works for tips, you deserve financial freedom; it is totally possible for you, and it's not too late!

So, whether you are here for a good time or a long time, if you earn tips you belong here. **Welcome.**

— Chapter One —
Please Wait to Be Seated

If they don't give you a seat at the table, bring a folding chair.

Shirley Chisholm

In order to get to the good stuff (aka, financial freedom), we need to first address the bad and the ugly. The fucked conditions surrounding tipped employment were designed a long time ago; tipped employment was created to benefit employers and leave employees out. I originally named this chapter "You are Excluded" as there are many very valuable employer-provided benefits which translate to tons of money you miss out on by being in the service industry (as opposed to working a typical nine-to-five job). These benefits and systems have continued to expand, creating a larger gap, and have left tipped workers further behind the starting line. However, you deserve better, so grab your folding chair, and hunker down for some hard truths.

In this chapter, we will look at what benefits you miss out on simply because you work in the service industry, why those benefits exist, and why you don't have access to them. In later chapters, we will break down all the ways you can recreate traditional benefits on your own, so you can get in on some of that life-changing magic. I ultimately changed the name of this chapter to "Please Wait to Be Seated" because while our society is not handing out invites to the wealthy table—in fact, society will tell you to get in line or that you don't meet the dress code—I want you to know that you *can* blow past the sign and pull up a chair. You *can* seat yourself, and even though there will be things you cannot do, you will get there by focusing on what you *can* do.

How It All Began

First, let's review the history of how the tipping culture for service industry workers started in the U.S. (because history matters, and we've been gaslit about tips for decades). The practice of tipped work started in Europe before the Civil War. Wealthier Americans brought the concept back from Europe thinking it was very aristocratic, but tipping saw an extremely problematic uptrend after the Civil War. Technically, liberated former slaves could not work for free any longer, so by saying they worked for tips, business owners and slave owners were able to capitalize on a loophole. Tipping became widely popularized as formerly enslaved people sought employment. For many, the only work they could find was in restaurants and on the railroad, which both were, at the time, tipped positions.

The tipping loophole allowed employers to not pay—and make additional profits on the backs of—their black, brown, uneducated, or minority employees. These individuals may have moved from "serving" in the home to working in public establishments, but the culturally held attitude that they—service workers—were "disposable" has remained at the forefront of the service industry. Rail workers eventually went on strike and received higher wages and eventually received benefits, but service workers still, to this day, are subject to a different minimum wage than all other workers and industries and are rarely offered what, by today's standards, is seen as a traditional benefits package.

Now, a note before we riot (which we totally should)—let's remember that the owners of many of today's establishments are not the same as those from the post-Civil War era. Most of these owners were tipped employees at one time who then took their passions for food, drinks, or entrepreneurship, along with their savings, and started their dream businesses. They wanted to do things their way, only to eventually realize that running a business in the service industry is very hard to operate successfully, which is likely why we haven't seen much disruption in employment trends.

    This is compounded by the fact that nine-to-five benefit administration and the compliance measures that come with administering things like 401(k)s, healthcare plans, and profit-sharing programs are extremely complicated and costly. For an industry with such a low success rate and large turnover factor, those benefits often don't make financial sense for employers, even the "good ones." In short, many employers simply would not know how to stay afloat if they had the added cost of an HR team or on-staff benefit person.

    It's important to note that while you, as a person, are irreplaceable, the flexibility in your shifts and hours, which is a huge draw for many, also means anyone your employer hires is capable of replacing you during your shift. Think about it—you love the fact you can switch shifts, and your boss knows anyone on their roster can take your place and still perform to make the business money. It's not a slight on you that anyone can fill in, but it's a perk and feature of the model of the industry you have chosen.

    For different industries where employee retention and their individual abilities and knowledge are vital to a company's success, employers create additional benefits that aim to keep employees from leaving and taking the training and intellectual properties to competitors. Those employers lose a lot of money with turnover. This is why benefit packages can vary so much from company to company—nine-to-five employers try to coax and retain employees they have already paid to train. Your service industry employer may not feel they need to do this because your skills are pretty transferable between employers; if you know how to bartend, it's pretty easy to find bartending work in many establishments. While that makes it easier for SIPs to land jobs across the industry, it also means you will work for employers that aren't driven to provide benefit packages. Keep this in mind as you continue reading; we will discuss ways for you to essentially replace what a benefit package would provide you (if you even were to have access to one, which, as a SIP, you probably don't).

Benefit Package Basics

In the last decade, we've seen many states make efforts to give tipped employees a living wage, as well as require employers with a certain number of employees to offer certain benefits. While we discuss the benefits that are generally not typical for SIPs, you may realize you are on the receiving end of some of them. We saw many employers struggle with finding and retaining staff post pandemic, and we started to see a shift into more and more traditional employer-provided benefits being added. While we are hopefully on an upward trend toward massive change in this industry, don't put that chair away just yet; it's a long way up.

Let's start by reviewing five of the most common employer benefits: paid time off, health insurance, retirement benefits, pre-tax benefits, and HR. It's important to understand how each of these benefits function because we will be recreating them for ourselves as part of our financial freedom strategy. There is also the possibility that you will one day be able to advocate for these benefits in your place of employment, in which case you will need some of this language. Let's dive in.

Paid Time Off

Paid time off, PTO, sick days, vacations days, personal time, or whatever you want to call it—most traditional employers include some paid time off or sick leave for their employees. However, for most tipped employees, this is not offered. Even if you are lucky enough to work in one of 19 states that, as of 2022, have some form of state or local law regarding sick time, you are unlikely to see much, if any, of that transfer to extra money on your check if you do take that time. For starters, you only receive minimum wage and are not compensated for tips lost as a result of your sick time, which means the bulk of your pay doesn't come your way when you take time off. Moreover, given that, as of the publication of this book, 40 out of 50 U.S. states pay tipped employees *less* than the federal—laughably paltry—minimum wage of $7.25 per hour, <u>with 22 of those states paying $2 and change an hour</u>, your check is hardly big money to begin with. Add to that the taxes taken out due to partial, forced, or full tip claiming, and many of us already typically see zero-dollar checks on the regular, making your "paid sick leave" a fantasy. Most people don't understand this and don't know that even if you "have the benefit" of PTO, cash-flow wise, you don't actually get a paid day off. However, this doesn't mean *you* shouldn't have a plan in place to support yourself when you need to take a sick day.

> *Example: The three doubles you worked in a row coupled with the four hours of sleep each night left your immune system weaker than the germs left on that used glass you cleaned up at the end of your last shift. You woke up the next morning feeling like death. Now what do you do—take an unpaid day off from work? Um, that isn't going to happen—you've got bills to pay, or your manager may write you up, so you take your sick ass to work, and you get all the other SIPs sick, too. When that cold turns into walking pneumonia, you end up in urgent care, or worse, the emergency room. What likely could have been a day or two at home and a few more days of taking it easy turns into two weeks of sickness and hundreds or thousands of dollars in medical expenses and lost wages. All this happened because you didn't have paid sick days, so you couldn't take a day off to go get that flu shot ahead of time or get that Z-Pak when you did start feeling it, so it got worse.*

If that sounds dramatic, it's only because we have been conditioned to think what our industry provides is adequate, when in fact it's not. Having real paid days off, ones for which you see the money on your check or in your hand the next week, is not only a financial benefit, but also a psychological one as well. Think about the fact that the average nine-to-five employee has 10 days of paid time off and an additional five days for sick leave, along with another five to seven paid holidays—that amounts to more than 20 paid days off a year. That is an entire working month. A month! Wouldn't you be a happier, healthier, more productive employee (hell, human!) if you got a paid month off each year?

If someone gave you a month's worth of wages, you would be ecstatic; it might even be life changing. Therefore, why are we so quick to accept that our positions exclude this benefit or that it's not that important of a benefit? If you had a month of days off, wouldn't you be able to forgo a ton of purchases you likely made to make your life easier? I'm thinking of you, to-go coffee! If I had 20 additional days off a year, I'd have the bandwidth to make my own coffee most weeks. Sick days are a huge safety net for employees, so they don't have to choose between caring for themselves or maintaining their financial lives. It's also a huge financial benefit. Add up a month of your tips. What would that equal? If you could pull from that bucket just for health-related expenses or just to take a day off, what would that look like? For me, it would have looked like going to the dentist a lot more regularly. I went almost 10 years without a dental visit, and I'm sure I don't have to tell you there were costly consequences that could have been avoided had I set aside $200 for a cleaning each year.

While paid sick days can cover for you when you're sick, what happens when you're just having a bad day, one of those days when you know if you go in to work, you will lose it? Taking it even further, have you ever abruptly quit a job—just walked out after or during a shift—and decided right then and there you were never going back? Unless something particularly atrocious happened that day, it was likely a result of burnout.

The small things built up—you got sick of the attitudes, the politics, the overscheduling, the under-scheduling, the power-tripping manager—and you decided you were done.

In the nine-to-five world, if you have a shit day or week and want to quit, you would likely tell yourself you can't just quit when you have paid vacation days available, and no way in hell are you going to leave that for the company, so you decide to schedule your vacation and coast until then. What typically happens is in the time leading up to your vacation, you get over the anger from that crap week, and when you finally do take that vacation, you come back refreshed, having realized maybe the grass isn't greener after all, and you can stick it out for a bit longer.

Because SIPs don't have a traditional vacation package, a hard deadline for when they have to take their PTO days by, or even a set of guidelines for how to take a vacation, this can mean you are less likely to take time off, putting you directly on the receiving end of burnout. The need for SIPs to relax and restore is real. Customer fatigue is real. Studies consistently find the highest stress jobs are ones that are incredibly demanding and allow for little control. Sound familiar? Having a portion of your compensation wrapped up in paid days off like nine-to-fivers do means being able to take time for your mental, physical, and emotional well-being. It encourages employees to step away from the grind of work. It's an employee "benefit" because it actually benefits the employees and keeps them coming back to work. Alternatively, the lack of PTO benefits for service industry roles means any time off is money lost, hardly a mental and emotional health builder. The bottom line is PTO days are a game changer, whether an employer provides them or you build them in for yourself.

Health Insurance

Healthcare goes hand in hand with PTO. You are on your feet hustling all day, every day, working the tray, the bottles, and the pole, and your body simply keeps on taking the hits. All of a sudden, you can't remember the last time you went to the doctor, let alone the dentist. Maybe you have health insurance through a spouse, or you are still able to get coverage on your parents' plan—if so, you are one of the lucky few. For the rest of the SIPs, even for those whose employers offer health insurance or those who found a plan through the Affordable Care Act, the health insurance options are often unaffordable, or the high deductibles prevent workers from utilizing the plan.

If we look at the past few years, the average nine-to-five employer paid 82 percent of their workers' healthcare premiums (roughly $6,000 per employee). As with PTO, this benefit has two implications. One is the money—what the benefit is worth. The second is the employee's health. When a person forgoes their annual exam or delays treatment or diagnostics testing due to financial reasons, there can be serious health consequences that may be irreversible.

We'll talk more about health insurance in Chapter 5, but just know that health insurance is a huge benefit—one that rightfully evokes a lot of passion and anger as the healthcare system in this country is overpriced and overly complicated. It's also a big reason many SIPs are forced to leave the industry—because they need coverage for themselves or a dependent due to an injury or illness.

Retirement Benefits

Retirement benefits encompass all the sources from which you can draw "income" to live off once you stop working. I know that sounds really far away and maybe super boring at this point, but traditional retirement can start as early as 59 years old. Given that the average life expectancy is currently 79 years old, there is a 20 year gap that we'll need our income covered. Trust that you will not want to be working because no one wants to be wrapping their achy legs around a pole five days a week at 60 years of age.

We're going to discuss a few different products and plans that have evolved over the past 100 years; it's important to understand the basics of each, so we know which ones we can have, how to get them, and how to grow them. This next part is a little dense, but don't skim! Push through, and reread where you need to. This is critical! It is the foundation to becoming financially free, which is the whole reason you're reading this book! I promise we will get to lighter and more fun stuff soon.

Pensions

Pensions came into existence in 1875. These are accounts employers set up and contribute money to on your behalf over your time at the company. The longer you work for the company and the higher your salary gets over the years, the more the monthly pension payment will be, and once you retire, you'll get monthly checks from that account for the rest of your life. The idea was that you give your working life to the company, and they will give you income throughout your "golden years."

Nowadays, unless you work for the government or a unicorn company, pensions are becoming obsolete, as they don't benefit employers as much as they once did (due to changing employment trends). Baby boomers and some Gen-Xers used to have 30- to 50-year careers with the same companies, but times have a changed. The average employee now stays with their employer for four-and-a-half years, so employers have replaced the pension with something called an employer-sponsored plan, such as a 401(k).

401(k)

Created in 1978, 401(k)s replaced many pensions and are now the staple for retirement accounts. These are employer-sponsored, which means employers are responsible for the setup costs and all the record keeping. Apart from real estate, a 401(k) is the number one way Americans build wealth!

Now, as a SIP, you may not be able to get a 401(k) through your employer, but that is no reason to run to the nearest desk job. You still have plenty of great retirement account options (which we'll discuss in Chapter 8). However, I'll admit it is hard to swallow that when Jason retires from his nine-to-five job, he will have $800,000 waiting for him, simply because he had someone named Sharon from HR who told him he needed to check a box on a piece of paper that put 10% of his paycheck into a workplace 401(k) account. And because it was automated, Jason never had to think about it, never had to feel as if he was losing money, and never had the option to spend it, which means 20 years from now, he will wake up and realize he can retire. Fuck Jason and his luck, and fuck the fact that we don't have our own Sharon. You can be your own Sharon from HR instead.[1]

Social Security

Nestled between the creation of the pension and the 401(k), which are both employer programs, is social security, created in 1935 by the government, which was their attempt to protect people who fell through the gaps and didn't have access to a pension or an employer-sponsored plan such as a 401(k). Guess who still falls through that gap? Yep! You guessed it—SIPs.

Social security is an income-based retirement program employees pay into when they claim their income. It looks like, and is generally thought of as, part of your "taxes." It is, in fact, a deduction from your check, just like your other taxes. It's important to note that it's both a deduction (now) and a benefit (later), but the benefit is only designed to replace a portion of your income, roughly 40 percent.

If you work at one of the ever-increasing number of establishments that report credit card tips for you, then most of your tips are being reported as income. Yay! Though hopefully they let you deduct your tip outs! However, when it comes to cash tips, or if you work somewhere that doesn't auto claim for you, you are probably used to self-reporting tips (aka, your income),

---

[1] For more on how to be your own Sharon, check out Appendix 3: How to Be Your Own Sharon.

so you have a lot of involvement and control in how much you contribute to social security. Whether you type it into the POS system when you clock out each shift, or you simply guess at tax time, I want you to think of tip claiming and income reporting as you funding your social security and a portion of the money you'll need for your future.

On the topic of tip reporting, you've probably had this thought: *Why would I report all my tips? At least half of it was in cash, and I had to tip out the house, the barback, and the bouncer. Why am I going to volunteer to pay taxes on the cash I received? I bet no one else I work with is doing that.* Or maybe you think claiming only a portion of your income is a huge perk of the job. I feel you on this. It's really easy to fall into this line of thinking, especially if you've never been given a crash course in the implications of not reporting all your income. But here's the truth: not reporting your tips can have serious implications for your future in regard to the potential social security payments you receive. The shocking and scary truth is that most retired SIPs rely *solely* on social security checks for survival. A super rough calculation of benefits would work out to just under half of what your average claimed income was.

> *Example: If you claim an average of $26,000 per year for 30 years, then at 65 years of age, you could see $12,000 in annual benefits, or $1,000 per month. Yikes! If you can't survive on that now, do you think you'll be able to do that at 65 years of age?*

Social security is completely based on the amount of money you claim to have earned. It's the IRS's way of giving back a portion of what you paid in taxes to help you in your retirement. If you aren't reporting all or a majority of your cash tips, that additional income reporting could add up to a large number, and that unreported income, over a long period of time, could significantly reduce the amount you stand to receive from the government when you will need it most.

The value of claiming all your tips doesn't start and stop with social security, either. It is not only future income you stand to receive by claiming your tips. First, if you ever plan on needing a mortgage or financing of any kind, one of the factors traditional lenders look for is W-2 income. The more of your tips you claim, the better you look on paper. So, if you plan to buy a home, car, or any other major purchase, you'll need to consider that banks can request W-2 and tax records to verify your income for the previous two years. Second, the single biggest factor to unemployment benefits is the income you were making at your previous employment. While the payout for unemployment isn't high, should you find yourself out of work, you'll be kicking yourself for not claiming all your tips. So, when it comes to claiming tips, do it. It's good for Future You. Also, it's the law. :)

Pre-Tax Benefits

Pre-tax benefits are something that, as a tipped person, you are already very familiar with and something we just touched on. If you get cash and don't report it to the IRS as income, then it is essentially pre-tax money because it hasn't been taxed, and that money is worth more because it has not had taxes deducted from it. It's bonus money!

> ### *Side Note*
> *It's also technically illegal not to claim all your tips, since it's not a qualifying pre-tax benefit.*

Pre-tax benefits that the government allows for are things such as employer-sponsored health and retirement plans that are deducted from paychecks *before* taxes are taken out. No fair! The average federal income tax is 15 percent, so for nine-to-fivers who get to pay their health insurance or retirement contributions with pre-tax money, it essentially means 15 percent more money going into their investments and a 15 percent discount on their health insurance, which, again, means less money is taxed and more money is put onto their checks. They get more in their retirement account and more money overall. SIPs don't have access to pre-tax benefits, unless you count unclaimed cash tips which, given the unfair nature of pre-tax insurance and retirement, who would blame you for not wanting to claim in full?

Human Resources

There is one group of people who knows these benefits better than most, and the nine-to-fivers have unlimited access to this resource—HR, aka, Sharon from the 401(k) example. Human resources is like a life coach that specializes in optimizing your workplace benefits and also encourages you to use them.

HR is the reason most nine-to-fivers invest in their workplace 401(k)s and are able to retire. HR employees are retirement heroes. The biggest tool they have at their disposal is automation, and when it comes to their employees' money, they do a great job of making sure some of it goes toward their futures.

They guide employees through the mess that is our healthcare system, and they are the people who make workers feel it's okay to take a day off.

HR normalizes talking about benefits; they normalize talking about retirement accounts, days off, and health insurance. When these things are discussed, and you see your peers utilizing them, you are more likely to participate.

Of course, on the other hand, HR will also drug test you, tell you that you can't hook up or flirt with your coworkers, and will write you up for 90 percent of the things you say when a guest is not around. These are probably some of the reasons HR is pretty scarce in the SIP environment.

Some of the employment benefits we reviewed may seem complex, or you may be asking yourself why we are reviewing benefits you can't have. Remember how I said we were excluded? Well, the first step to getting you a seat at the table is understanding why SIPs are among the most economically disadvantaged in our country. How can you advocate for something you don't yet know you need? It is these benefits and systems that are responsible, at least in part, for wealth building for the majority of Americans.

The money world is complex, and taxes are complex (even for people with a Sharon supporting them). The important thing is that you are starting to familiarize yourself with both the language and the concepts. I remember working at a very fancy sushi restaurant in Boston, and the chef wanted us to understand and be able to explain all the dishes and their ingredients. It was like another world, and it took me quite a long time—weeks of studying the menu, Googling ingredients, making note cards, and simply hanging out in the kitchen—before I got a handle on it. Stick with it, even if you feel lost, because you will eventually have your "aha" moments, and they will be glorious, just like the tips I got from that sushi restaurant. At the end of the day, even the best investors admit they have no idea why the markets move, but they still show up and invest every day.

> ### *Financial Freedom Road Map Steps*
>
> *Welcome to your very first Financial Freedom Road Map Steps! At the end of each chapter, we will list some relevant action steps for you to take on your way to financial freedom. Consider these steps as reminders and guidance on how you can get the most out of each chapter and the book as a whole. The most important thing you can do while reading this book is to take consistent action, one step at a time.*
>
> - Find out what benefits your employer provides. It's possible your employer forgot to mention some of their benefits or possible it didn't register at the time you were hired. Do yourself a favor and check in. My favorite way to ask this is by saying, "My friend is thinking about applying here and wanted me to ask if we offer any employer benefits."

PLEASE WAIT TO BE SEATED

- Check your state's requirements for employers. Google "do [your state] employers have to offer health insurance," and then do the same for PTO. While you're at it, confirm your state's tipped minimum wage.

— Chapter Two —

Front of House, But Back of Mind

*I am not a product of my circumstances.
I am a product of my decisions.*

Stephen Covey

On the surface, it's starting to sound as though we chose the wrong industry to work in—nine-to-fivers get all the benefits, and we're stuck with zero-dollar paychecks. After the last chapter, you may even be thinking about retiring your G-string or apron for good. It's true that SIP employment varies widely on paper from the nine-to-five world. I can try to buffer this next part by reminding you how much you love getting cold hard cash, that you love hitting up the beach on a random Tuesday, and that you can have some serious fun with your guests, but there's one more area we need to compare before we can move on to the good stuff (how you can be a financially free SIP on your own terms)—our physical space. The setup of our pay and benefits is only half of the equation. What about location, setting, and how we move through our work?

Our environment influences every aspect of our lives, but it especially influences our financial lives. We often think we control all our decisions. This is only true to a certain extent and only when we honestly examine our lives for those influences. It is the examined environment, the one we reflect on, that allows for the most intentionality and control. In this chapter, we will look at influences of a SIP environment, how those influences may affect our spending and our lifestyles, and how paying greater attention to those influences will lead to better decision making and a better bottom line.

In a lot of industries, there are known hazards you must be cautious of. For example, in construction, the hazards are pretty straightforward: each day construction workers are surrounded by dangerous equipment, heights, and chemicals that can injure them. However, hazards in the mental health field are a bit different. As a therapist, you would get additional training to know how to avoid having your patients fall in love with you. The environment of therapy involves a lot of vulnerability, sharing, listening, teamwork, and appreciation, elements not dissimilar from those that are found within desirable romantic relationships. It's easy and common for transference to occur. In short, workers get training in order to avoid some of the more dangerous aspects of their jobs. Cross-training is often advised to make an employee more likely to foresee and avoid hazards.

SIPs' places of employment have hazards, too, but often, only the physical ones are discussed. Most of us know we need to change out of our uniforms, so we don't look like targets walking out of our establishments late at night, exhausted from our shift, potentially with large wads of cash. If we are walking to our cars, we know to do it as a group or with a security guard. We also know not to give out too much personal information to our guests. But what about all the other hazards to our mental safety, our confidence, our financial security, and our health? Let's look at the hazards in the service industry that impact those facets of our lives.

Guests

Guests can, in fact, be workplace hazards—hazards to our mental health, hazards to our confidence, and hazards to our grasp on reality. How many times have you heard from a guest, "Do you have a real job? What do you want to do for your career? What's next after this?" Sometimes our guests have a way of chipping at our confidence, our choices, and our self-respect. Some do it out of concern, some out of jealousy, and some because they are poor-mannered pricks. And as much as we say, "Fuck 'em," we are social creatures who crave acceptance, and those digs can add up and turn into self-loathing or making poor decisions to numb it all out. People can suck, and they can say shitty, hurtful things when they are trying to decompress or connect, and you have to find a healthy outlet to deal with this workplace hazard in a way that does not compromise your tips or your safety.

How do you build your self-esteem back up? You are doing it right now! A great way to build up your confidence and self-esteem is by investing time into yourself. Do it by reading or learning something new. Do it by getting exercise. Do it by making plans for the future. Do it by setting yourself up for success. *Don't* do it by leaning into habits that drain your resources, such as buying expensive shoes or taking three shots of tequila.

You can also support yourself by learning how to engage with guests in a more self-protective way. For example, let's go back to when a guest asks what your real job is. I know we all have a host of answers we would rather give, and we usually have a rotation of answers we *actually* give, depending on how the interaction with that guest has gone so far. After reading this book, you may choose not to share your new financial strategy or may choose to bluntly say, "I'm taking the money you rude assholes are giving me, and it's going to make money while you sleep, so in 10 years, while you are sitting in your ivory tower living beyond your means, I'll be living my best life."

Instead, you may want to craft a handful of responses ahead of time that feel true and don't demean yourself or your job; this will only add to your armor. Using self-deprecating humor or putting down your profession or place of employment to agree with a guest is not only bad for your mental health, but it also perpetuates shame and stereotypes throughout the industry. So, instead of cracking a joke about moving out of your parents' basement or "getting out of here in a few months," you could say something like, "I'm a very opportunistic person, and I'm working hard while keeping my eyes open for the next big thing, so my fingers are crossed. Plus, I got to meet you!" as you smile and walk away.

Alcohol

Another hazard that is often seen as a perk of the SIP environment is alcohol, so buckle up for this double-edged sword because we are going there. The SIP industry is one of socialization and drinking, sometimes to excess. No shame and no judgment. Our industry is based on alcohol, which is a hazard, and as with all hazards, we need to know how to protect ourselves. For the most part, you are surrounded by people who are drinking. All day long, you are shown examples of people socializing over cocktails, relaxing with beers, laughing and getting excited over margaritas, going on dates with martinis, looking fabulous and dressed up over champagne, and eating delicious food with red wines, but most importantly, we see people *not* working when drinking cocktails. It's honestly a huge surprise to me that more SIPs aren't raging alcoholics, though our industry's numbers are among the worst. Our biggest example of people living life and having fun is in the presence of constant alcohol. I'm not here to have an opinion on alcohol in general, but this is a big difference in the work environments of SIPs, so we will look at it from a few angles. Make sure you're honest with yourself as you think about it because no one is watching or judging.

The Cost of Recovery

Alcohol is appealing, and it's a big part of the money we all depend on. I can't tell you how many shifts I worked tipsy, drunk, or hungover. When I moved to New York, I started out working as a Coyote—yes, from the movie *Coyote Ugly*. Yes, it exists, and yes, it's really like that... Well, it used to be. The shifts there required a *lot* of drinking, and I often stumbled home at 6 a.m. I have a lot to say about my Coyote days, but when it comes to the financial aspects, while the shifts were incredibly profitable, one of the costs I didn't consider at the time was that I was spending the majority of the next day in bed, hungover, on my day off! I confused recovering with relaxing, and that lost time was a cost of working. While I bragged to my friends that I made over a thousand dollars the night before, what I failed to mention was there were another two days I was severely hungover and feeling totally out of it. How many days of the year are you hungover due to work or because of necessary decompressing? It's a cost of working in this environment.

The Cost of Winding Down

There are the physical tolls of drinking and the constant pull and appeal of alcohol due to our environment, but what about the financial costs? How much do you personally spend on alcohol? Sure, there is something very cathartic about sharing stories from a bad shift over a few cocktails, but how often are you doing that? Once a week? More? And how much are these outings costing you? This is another cost of working—the cost of winding down. One of the financial bibles, *Your Money or Your Life*, by Vicki Robin, dives deep into the costs associated with working. The author calculates what each item costs her based on her time to work for it, and since we all have a limited number of hours in our lives, she says this focus helps people live and spend with their values and purpose in mind.

Winding down after a shift, because of the shift, is a work expense. So, what are you spending when you say, "Ugh, I had a shit day, and I need a drink. Want to go next door?" and spending three hours of your life complaining about the crappy guests you had that day (a process you'll repeat again and again on future bad days)? Have you ever added it up? Does one post-shift vent session make up the earnings of one of your shifts? More than one shift? And if so, are you okay with trading hours of your hard work, only to complain about work and to drink that money away?

Example: Let's do the math. For one three-hour wind down, let's assume you'll have three margaritas with good tequila because you have to work tomorrow and don't want a hangover, chips, guac, and queso. That's easily a $60 bill, a relatively mild night out for SIPs. Then you have three hours of your time, which, for ease, let's just say would net you another $60 (though it's likely far more than that). That means you just spent $120 to work that week (or that night).

If you are anything like me, this scenario happens multiple nights a week. If you add up the amount of money you spend in a year socializing after your shift, would you feel good about your decision? Or, would you realize that if you kept the after-work outings to a minimum, you could have used that money for a portion of a down payment, a big vacation, or a new-to-you used car?

Many of us stick our heads in the sand and don't want to know how much we spend on these outings in a year because deep down, we know that if we actually saw a hard number for how much we spent, we'd want to cut it down. One problem with the "ignore it totally or get rid of it all" line of thinking is most people are making the wrong comparison. You may be saying to yourself, "If I knew how much I spent, then I would feel too guilty to continue going out multiple nights a week, and I like going out, and if I had to choose between going out and not going out, well I would choose going out." What if you said this instead: "Last year I spent $10,000 dollars on coffee, dining out, and drinking (or $192 a week). Instead, I'm going to limit myself to $40 a week ($2,000 per year). With the $8,000 difference, I'm going to max out my IRA for the year and go to Mexico."

The question becomes would you rather not think about your money and let it go out into the world whenever your coworkers want you to spend money, *or* would you rather set yourself up for retirement, go to Mexico for a vacation, *and* still go out once a week for a few drinks? Intentionality is all about *you* and what you want. It is about making choices that support your goals. You *don't* always want to spend your hard-earned money mere hours after it's entered your life.

Now, look, I get it. I'm expecting to hear some serious complaints for this chapter: "But Barbara, one of the joys of working in the service industry is the social aspect; I'm building friendships and investing time into better working relationships that can later assist me financially." "But Barbara, if I wanted to listen to someone question my drinking habits, I'd call my mother." "But Barbara, if I didn't go out with my work people I'd still be going out with my friends." "But Barbara, after a long day of slinging drinks, don't I deserve a nice drink?" We might as well call this the "But Barbara" chapter, because I've heard it all, and you're not all wrong!

The fact is that sometimes a SIP shift is super energizing, and you need to burn off a little steam after some big rushes. Maybe you didn't get time to have any watercooler talk because it was a really busy shift. Maybe you are allowed to drink at your establishment, so you roll up to the bar because you were cut early, and you want to wait for the rest of the team to finish up, so you can spend some time together. It may be true that some of the people you work with will become your lifelong friends, but historically, that is not the case. People move on to different employers, people change industries, and the cycles start over. You are left with a huge circle of acquaintances, which is great, but I wish I had saved that money and put it into a few special people—or better yet, into myself and my future self. Future You is who deserves it.

Have you ever heard the expression "the cobbler's kids have no shoes"? I'm sure there is another point to this fable and expression, but my takeaway was that when you are constantly surrounded by something you deal with all day long, it is pretty fucking annoying to have to do it for yourself. If you make shoes all day, then the last thing you want to do is make your kids shoes. If you are a CPA, the last thing you want to do is file your own taxes; if you are a bartender, sometimes you just want someone else to make a finely crafted cocktail for you after a long hard day. I'm not telling you to give up your cocktails, but I am telling you that if you were in a different field, you'd probably find yourself going home and pouring yourself a glass of wine from a $12 bottle, rather than paying for a $12 glass.

One of the consequences of being a super-star hospitality person is that the training and experience you've received has made you the ultimate consumer. Your pallet is extremely refined from years of whiskey or wine tasting, and you know the $25 bottle is probably better than the $2 one, and the $80 bottle is likely better than the $25 one. You taste the premium ingredients and distinct notes and know the backstory of how the company got started and how the product is manufactured. It only makes sense that you want and crave better-than-average products. You may need to remind yourself that all that tasting has also given you the information to know which one of all the $12 bottles of wine is the best, and more importantly, you know the markup on booze is crazy high. Maybe it's better to use that knowledge to find what value is best for you.

Narcotics

Another hazard of the job is the exposure to narcotics. I worked at a dive bar in Las Vegas, an actual "OG" dive bar, called Lucky's Tavern. It was located between a truck stop gas station and a motel that allowed you to rent rooms by the hour. The clientele was a mix of working women, truck drivers, and locals. The perk of the job and the reason I stayed was that my boss let me keep the money for every shot I was able to get someone to buy me, as long as I poured my shot with my "special bottle," a bottle of Jägermeister with a signature rubber band around the neck of the bottle, that I had filled with flat coke. I made a lot of money doing that. The ladies wanted company when there were no drivers around, and once the drivers came in, it was a party until last call. While I was there, I was offered every drug under the sun. Many of the drivers had uppers to keep them going, and many of the locals preferred downers.

Drugs, alcohol, and tobacco are all different products, but they are all indulgences, ones that have similar addictive and financial properties. Drugs and tobacco, as with alcohol, are incredibly costly, and if you are a habitual or recreational user of either, I highly encourage you to plug the costs of your monthly habit into a compound calculator to see how much a 30-year habit will cost you.[1] As with alcohol, these two items are typically around the establishments where SIPs work, and in my experience, most people partaking in drugs and tobacco are also adding drinks to the mix.

If I'm starting to sound like a vanilla narc, let me reassure you that I am, and was, far from it. However, one of the main regrets I have is that I let my surroundings and the "YOLO" vibes that come with being a SIP prevent me from seeing the truth. Many of the people who were out drinking or coming into my place of employment had safety nets in place that came before their outings and habits (savings, employer benefits, regular salaries, etc.). Those nets didn't diminish the fun they had when they were there, and when their money ran out, those nets were still in place. It's an important distinction: on far too many evenings, we *spend what we have*, whereas non-SIPs would *spend what they have left over*.

SIP environments mess with our perception of the world and how we live. In our jobs, we are shaping experiences; we are selling fun and a feeling of being carefree. Those experiences are also shaping us, our expectations, and our assumptions for how to live life. They give us prescriptions for what is important. It is in taking an honest look at our spending habits, our choices in how we spend our time, and who we surround ourselves with that we can see how we are constantly influenced by the people we see and serve in our work environments. Luckily, we have the power to put systems—including our own short- and long-term goals—in place to help reduce how much our environment influences our behavior.

Most importantly, this is about building up an awareness, taking note of the overt or subtle ways your career has been

---

[1] Check out the compound calculator resource in Appendix 4.

affecting and shaping how you spend your money, as well as taking note of what you currently value. Your environment affects how you spend, but it also affects how you earn and the attitudes you hold about the money coming to you. In the next chapter, we will look at the earning side of the equation.

> ## Financial Freedom Road Map Steps
>
> *Take these mindful action steps to understand how your environment is messing with your money, so you can increase your control and move yourself closer to financial freedom!*
>
> - Think of the worst things your guests have said to you about yourself, your job, or your place of employment. Write down a response or two that are respectful of you, your profession, and your place of employment, one that feels true and positive. Keep those statements in mind when you talk to your guests.
> - Identify the financial hazards in your workplace. Make a list of all the things that may be tripping up your financial life. What would it look like if you put protection measures in place, such as stronger boundaries (with co-workers, guests, or friends) or self-imposed barriers or rules? Example: "I don't go out after shifts over the weekend."
> - Add up how much money you spend to work each week (include the cost of winding down, work outings, food, clothing, beverages, Ubers home, shifts you don't pick up or that you release because you are hungover, etc.). Review how many hours you have to work to pay that off (how many hours you have to work to pay to work). How do you feel when you see that number multiplied by 52? How could you better allocate your money and time?

— Chapter Three —

You're a Hustler; Hustle Responsibly

Hustle is about understanding and working the spaces and angles between what is obvious to everyone else, and using those quiet moments to stand out. To win. That is the hallmark of a true hustler.
Taraji P. Henson

The goal of financial freedom looks different for everyone, but the driving themes for most are security and choice. Security is what you need to survive, and choice is what you need to be happy. Security is planning and preparing for your future, and choice is planning and preparing for the present. Security can look like buying a home or investing for your later stages of life. Choice can look like the freedom to switch jobs or taking a few weeks off. Security can look like a retirement account, whereas choice can look like an emergency fund (more on both of those later). Both security and choice are about money, the money you make, and, more importantly, the money you keep. Before we get into how to keep it and where to put it, we need to talk about the money coming in, how you earn, and how your attitudes about earning it will be pivotal in pursuing financial freedom.

The Power of the Hustle

There are not a lot of industries where you can work more to make more. While you currently may be trading time for money, you still possess the power to turn hustle into money, and that is where financial freedom starts. Hustle is a state of flow, a vibe, an energy, a mindset; and you may be surprised to learn that most nine-to-fivers don't have it and can't grow it like you do. The hustle you possess is about you spotting opportunities within your day. You may be juggling mountain-sized problems along with 20 guests, but you always somehow manage to figure it out. It's this hustle mentality that makes you someone who can achieve big goals.

Hustle has turned into a problematic word in some circles as it can be used to represent a toxic culture, a lack of healthy boundaries, and unrealistic or inappropriate expectations—such as working harder, faster, and stronger. It's used a lot in the nine-to-five world where exempt employees (salaried employees) are asked to complete projects that will take much more time and energy than their 40-hour work week. With promises of exposure, experience, or advancement, their hustle is about working after hours, being available at all times, and getting ahead of their peers—all for the same salary.

When others ask for or expect hustle, it can be harmful. Our hustle, however, is self-defined. In a lot of ways SIPs are their own bosses, and our hustle means utilizing and amplifying our skills, while working and finding unique opportunities or ways to optimize what we currently have to work with; it never means sacrificing wellness. The work of young and developing individuals is to learn boundaries, no matter the industry. That being said, always hustle to the beat of your own drum, and always hustle responsibly.

Identifying the Hustle

Not sure if you're a hustler? Let me lay out some common scenarios to see if you recognize yourself in any of these. It's a slow month at work. Maybe you didn't get many shifts on the schedule, but you've figured out a way to pick up some extra shifts. No one wants to give up shifts during that time, so you have to get creative; maybe you offer to let them borrow that item that they've had their eye on. Maybe you offer to pet sit, offer to bring them coffee every day for the next week, or maybe you know you can make $250 on that shift, so you offer them $50 to let you take it. Perhaps you've persuaded your manager to make cuts early, or you've found ways to keep patrons in their seats longer by playing games. Anytime you are going beyond the required script, you are hustling, and it's a benefit to everyone.

Up until now, you've likely done your hustle to cover your bills or to buy new things. However, we will start to look at our hustle as a means to buy our choice and security. That being said, remember this—the money made in the service industry can become addictive. This new mindset about the hustle is for setting and achieving goals, not to run you ragged. Don't forget to take the hustle hat off occasionally and plug into some R&R.

There are many ways to use the hustle to your advantage. Let's take a look at a few of the other simple ways you may already, or can, be hustling to achieve your goals.

Multiple Jobs

I had more than one job for the majority of my time in the industry, and while sometimes it was a lot to juggle in terms of scheduling and coordination, it did solve many of the problems we discussed in Chapter 2. For example, I remember a time when I was waiting tables at a fine dining establishment while also bartending at a dive bar. The contrast of the environments and the guests was my saving grace when one extreme got to be too much. Another time, I was dancing at a club and working at a sports bar, and when summers were slow at the club, I could lean into playoffs at the sports bar job, which was also a win-win for the management at the sports bar.

The other aspect I liked was the diversification. If something bad was happening at one job, I took solace in my other job. If things were slow in one spot, I could count on income from the other job. Multiple jobs are not for everyone, and if what you're doing now with one job is enough, and it has the room to add more hustle, so you can put money into your choice and security funds, then there's no need to mess up a good thing. But, if you've ever been curious about holding multiple jobs, then I encourage you to sit with the idea and think about how that could work for you.

Managing Management

Maybe you've been thinking about a second job for some time, but you are too scared to change your availability or have that conversation with a current manager to make room for that second job. It's often easier to ask for more shifts than it is to ask for less or more specific shifts. If that is the case for you, and you think you may need to add a different job to the mix, try carving out small boundaries first. For example, perhaps you could ask your manager, "Can we talk about six months from now? I want to get your buy-in on how I could start taking Mondays off." Generally, if you approach management openly, honestly, and with the establishment's needs in mind, you will find success.

Of course, there will always be managers who take such changes or mere thoughts of changes rather personally. Insecure managers can view your desire to split your time as an attack on their own choices—"I've chosen this place full time. So should you." They may also be the type of manager who leverages their approval as a management tactic, so they rely on you more and have an easier job for themselves. If that is the culture, or if the culture is even more controlling or potentially borderline abusive, then you may want to think about whether that's the type of environment that will allow you to grow. We are talking about freedom, choice, and security in this book. That means you have to be an active participant in making sure you are in environments where you can have agency and choice. If the environment is not malleable and capable of aligning with your goals, you need to start looking for something else.

Tackling management could be its own book, but as a hustler, you know management is a resource, so work to best position yourself with that resource. You know management is the key to getting good shifts and being able to grow in an establishment. Politicking is one angle, but I've always been a bigger fan of letting my interests and my hustle lead during my shifts. It takes less energy, and, frankly, it means the focus is more on you individually. The fact that you bought this book shows you are someone who takes initiative, and you are always looking for more ways to showcase it. Ask for new challenges, or ask for a shift to train on service bar or center stage. Some call it brownnosing; I call it hustling. We will use that extra effort of focusing on getting more income to help us grow our choice and security funds.

We Got Skills

In addition to challenging management, we deal with some strange people, strange requests, and strange scenarios on a pretty consistent basis, both with our coworkers and with our guests. Our environment is constantly changing, and because of this, we have developed a series of skills that aid in the hustle. These include the following:

- **We got mad listening skills.** Constant interaction with new people has helped us develop genius level listening skills. A big part of our job is paying attention and really hearing what other people are saying. Listening *is* our foundation skill.
- **We are good at empathy**, even if we need to fake it occasionally or a lot.
- **We excel at communicating** in general, mirroring, and making ourselves likable or relatable to different audience types, sometimes at the same time a mere few seats away from one another. This includes both verbal and nonverbal communication.
- **We are good at getting people to trust us** and to be vulnerable with us.

- A hustler is extremely adept at reading the room. **We take inventory** (literally and figuratively) and keep our resources in the back of our minds. We know when to play what card. We know which guests need more of our time and which need less.
- **We also are stacked with intrapersonal skills**, especially at work. When we know our wheelhouse, we are confident, patient, self-motivated, and we can put any guest at ease.
- **We rock at time management.** From knowing how long it takes to course or stage meals to how long until a seat will turn, we understand how to manipulate our surroundings to meet time demands and how to set proper expectations for our patrons, so we can exceed those expectations. We know how to churn if needed. For me, a lot of when I feel I am in flow is when I am nailing time management, and it's in that excellence and mastery I feel the most joy.

These are all skills people pay a lot of money to learn at places like Harvard Business School—skills many professionals fail to adopt. For SIPs, we do it so frequently it's become second nature, and we forget they are skills, and we are awesome at the people game, which, in every type of business, is half of any position. These skills come from, and help to further, our hustle. Not only do they help us increase our tips and income, but they also will serve us on our journey in anything we want to do.

You are awesomely skilled, and we need to talk about it because as SIPs, we stare down society's judgment on a daily basis, all while serving them and making them feel good about themselves. We often don't see the skills we have gained from the many and varied situations we are put in. We take our skill sets for granted and assume others with more formal educations or "proper" work experience have more marketable skills. This feeling is called "imposter syndrome" (where we feel like a fraud, despite our obvious skills and experience), and everyone has it. I'm serious; everyone has it. It's important to call out and name our imposter syndrome, because when we start talking about our goals—saving for retirement, saving an emergency fund, or investing—you may think, *I have no idea what I'm doing*, or, *I'm not someone who can retire*, or, *I can't save that amount of money*. All of those thoughts are your imposter syndrome talking, and that nasty little syndrome is wrong because you are highly skilled, highly capable, and you have hustle.

Hustle, Even When You're Down

Despite our overwhelming skills, a surprising aspect of hustling is failing. It's a critical component of the resilience you demonstrate and also a big part of the learning process. We fail often, such as when you forget to ring in a table's order, when you drop a bottle of really expensive wine, or when you kick a patron in the face and cause a giant gash on their head with a seven-inch stiletto heel (you know, just a general failure. Not one in particular that I have an exceptionally acute memory of or anything…). The point is, we all fail.

Failing and recovering is part of what makes SIPs well situated to start down the path of financial freedom. You understand what it's like to break down your thinking and start from scratch. You can handle disappointments and know you have the ability to forgive yourself for screwing up. This is critical for getting back on the horse again. If you are still working on the forgiveness portion or hiding some of your shameful mistakes, I encourage you to bring those bad boys out into the light. We all fail, and we all are messy, and only after tackling the giant shame monster can we start down the road to forgiveness and recovery. As Brené Brown (best-selling author and the world's foremost researcher on shame and empathy) points out, "Shame hates it when we reach out and tell our story. It hates having words wrapped around it—it can't survive being shared. Shame loves secrecy. When we bury our story, the shame metastasizes." If we share our feelings on our failings, then they cannot develop into shame and won't keep us from hustling our way to financial freedom.

Our ability to work well under pressure and handle timely and stressful situations on a daily basis is very impressive. Sure, maybe you've cried once or twice in the bathroom or walk-in cooler, but who hasn't? You're on stage or behind the bar when a fight breaks out. You catch some illicit or dangerous acts going on in your place of employment. You react swiftly, calmly, and with the temperament of a fucking majestic swan. You instantly have a handle on the situation and can act in the best interest of the company.

If you do ever decide to leave the service industry, then you need to remember that all of your experience is valuable to employers in other sectors. If you are the bold type, you can always lead by reminding the interviewer that if they want another fresh college graduate with no previous job or life experience, there will be a hundred of them, all exactly the same, to choose from, but if they want someone who can spot opportunities, someone who can deal with all types of personalities, someone adept at problem solving and multi-tasking, and someone who can think outside the box, then they should really consider hiring you. Now, don't get me wrong. I'm not telling you that you should leave the service industry, but I need you to know that your skill set game is strong, and anyone would be lucky to have you. You are a hustler—can't stop, won't stop.

Upping the Hustle

Now that you remember what a magically exceptional human you are, let's talk strategy. Whether you are brand new to the industry and need a little more clarity on how to apply this hustle attitude, or you're a lifer who simply needs a reminder that the tried-and-true tactics really do work, let's review the classic dos and don'ts, so you can boost your hustle and your income.

- **DO: Be open and ready for guests at all times.** Picture the scenario. You are working the bar on a lunch shift. A guest walks in. They are hungry and have only 30 minutes. If you are standing behind the bar in a position closest to the door with a menu in your hand, and you are the first person to make eye contact and greet them, then you stand a much better chance of having that guest at your bar—and we all know bar theory: people are more likely to sit at a bar when people are already sitting there.
- **DON'T: Hide out in the back.** If you're in the back chatting while the hostess tries to hunt you down, you will miss out on opportunities. The money is walking in the front door. Be the closest person to the money.
- **DO: Build out your regulars.** Creating community and experiences is what being in this industry is all about. You will make more money if people know you, like you, and feel you are grateful to have them. They can get the goods anywhere; you (and how you make them feel) are what makes the experience unique. There are a lot of ways to build out regulars based on the establishment and your role, but make a plan. How can you get someone to return and ask for you? Do you make them feel special by remembering their name, drink, or story? Did you comp them a drink, score them free fries, or make them laugh after they had a bad day? Did you entertain them with tricks or stories of your own?

  Maybe you are a hairstylist, and this month, you want to focus on customer relations. Take a photo of your clients at the end of their services. Buy a bottle of product and send clients home with free samples. It's one final way of saying their image is important to you. Maybe you are a valet attendant; one way to improve customer relations could be purchasing a small whisk broom and using it to dust off the seat before you hand over the keys, another way of saying, "I cared for your car." These small extra steps of service keep people tipping and coming back, and they will move you to the top level of mastery, which is something that will always benefit you in the long run. As someone brilliant once said, "Whatever you are, be a good one."

- **DO: Grow your skills.** There are always ways you can improve, so keep a growth mindset. When I started out pole dancing, I would work on one new trick combination every night I worked. It would be three or four movements I would switch the order of throughout the night. Work is not only the place where you display what you've already mastered, but it's also a live training session. Get comfortable with growing in front of people because the only person you should ever compete with is yourself. How can you be better than you were last month or last year?
- **DO: Take on more responsibility.** At some point, you may have the opportunity to manage, train, or delegate. If your general manager (GM) asks you to become a manager, and you really don't want to (it's very possible you are making more money on the floor), don't completely shut it down. Explain to the GM why managing isn't right for you right now, or ask if there is potential for a hybrid role.
- **DO: Offer your manager an alternative.** Okay, so maybe managing doesn't speak to you, but perhaps being an hourly supervisor or lead who can still collect tips does appeal to you. Rather than turning down an opportunity, hustle and turn it into the opportunity you want. There is no harm in asking and being confident, positive, and creative with presenting solutions to your GM; this is exactly why they thought of you in the first place!
- **DON'T: Be the weakest link.** We all know the saying about how you are only as good as your worst worker. This is so true for people in the hospitality industry. You rely on your kitchen staff, your runners, your security, your barbacks, your DJ, your bussers, and your cleaning staff, to name a few. If you rely on someone else's

work to make you money, then you need to show your appreciation appropriately.

I once heard a story about a Harvard professor who taught a business class. His class was tough, and it was rumored that passing the class meant acing the final exam. The final exam consisted of only one question: Write down the name of the janitor who has cleaned this room immediately following every class for the entire semester. We all have an important role, and that needs to be respected.

- **DON'T: Skimp on tip out.** Your support staff are the people who run to change kegs for you, keep watch and provide security for you, or clean your tables, so you have better turnover. Just as you get offended or irritated when someone doesn't tip you what you deserve, so do your coworkers when you decide your bottom line is more important than your integrity. If you get a reputation as someone who doesn't tip out appropriately, then there is no incentive for those people to work hard for you. If you are someone who shares equitably, then when you do have a bad night, those workers will be more understanding when their share is also less than usual.
- **DO: Upsell.** Ugh, I hate this word and had a serious aversion to the concept for a long time. A while back, I was working in Las Vegas at a bar. I worked for a young guy named David. He had just bought the bar and read too many books on entrepreneurship. He was so blinded by his ability to own a bar in Las Vegas that he lost sight of his core clientele. He tried to apply his theoretical concepts to our standards of service at a dive bar. I remember one time he brought in a script. Apparently, he figured the reason his business wasn't growing as fast as he wanted was because his bartenders weren't saying the right sequence of words. The new script included some of these sentences: "How about a pack of Reds for the road?" or, "Would you like a slice of

ooey-gooey cheese pizza to go with your PBR?" I hated upselling for a good number of years after.

A few years after I got over my PTSD with upselling, I was working in that upscale sushi restaurant in Boston. I worked weekends at the bar and cocktail lounge and made an average of $800 a night. I made that all through the art of upselling. I upsold Saki bottles, Omakase, desserts, coffee, and private chef experiences that I made up. I once asked John Mayer if he wanted to walk through our kitchen. Ting San was not too happy with that, but I learned the value of leverage, exclusivity, and experience as a way to maximize what you have. You may only have one-dollar slices of cheese pizza and Jäger, or you may have the world's finest blowfish sashimi and Dom Perignon. As much as you may think it's about what you have, the focus should be on what you can do with what you have. Upselling is a very good strategy for increasing your check average, which is a great strategy for increasing your income. Know the top-tier items on your menu and how to describe them. If the kitchen is open to it, craft off-menu items to create some allure. Find ways to create add-ons.

- **DON'T: Be afraid of management.** The standard of service that is set by management represents a minimum. Talk with your manager if you have ideas about how to earn more. Even if they shoot down your ideas or don't have any of their own, you've demonstrated you are motivated, and that can go a long way. If the idea is shot down, ask if you could test the idea for one night, or ask if they would consider allowing you to take a poll. After all, they aren't having one-on-one conversations with the regulars; you are. Leverage your expertise.
- **DO: Ask for more.** If you have done all the above suggestions, then it might be time to talk to your manager about increasing your hourly wage. An often overlooked way to increase your income is to ask for an increase in your hourly rate. Your employer is not required to stick to

the minimum wage, but, of course, they do. Why would they voluntarily give up more of their profit? Maybe you work at an establishment that pools tips, but if you find yourself on all of the heavy lifting shifts, an adjustment to your hourly wage may be the only way to provide you additional compensation. If you are making money for the business in a proven and measurable way, speak to your manager and try to negotiate a pay raise. Even if your check is mostly or totally eroded by taxes after the increase, it is still an added benefit. The hourly wages in your paycheck cover some of the money you owe for taxes. Therefore, the higher your paycheck, the more taxes it will cover, which means, overall, more money in your pocket or G-string.

Tip for the Tipped

How to negotiate your hourly salary:

- Make a list of all the ways you go above and beyond in your role—be specific and list examples. If you cannot recall anything specific, or frankly, even if you can, start a running list. You can keep a notes file on your phone—a gold star list. After your shift, record any examples of going the extra mile. If you do this, you'll always have it at the ready!
- Make your pitch a win-win. Your employer gets to show that good employees are valued and rewarded, and it strengthens the commitment you have to them. If your employer is hesitant or concerned about how it would look to other employees, ask if there is a way to create a position like a shift lead that would justify the increase.
- See if there are additional responsibilities or things you may be able to take off your manager's plate. Maybe you take on the worst side work, or perhaps you can help with inventory, scheduling, or training of new employees.

Control Your Hustler Lifestyle

Now that we're clear on how being a hustler is a key asset for any SIP, and we've identified the pros, tips, and tricks of the hustle, we have to look at the other side of the coin. Alas, every rose has its thorn. One of the arch nemeses to the hustler lifestyle is wasteful spending. "Lifestyle creep" is another name for what we are trying to avoid. In the nine-to-five world, it would be when your friend, who has consistently received raises in her career and makes $100,000 a year, is constantly broke. Each time she received a raise, she went out to brunch for a few weeks in a row to celebrate, she upped her wardrobe, she booked an epic vacation, or she moved into a slightly better apartment. All that spending, and whoops, there goes her raise—and then some—as she tries to keep up with the newer and bigger lifestyle.

When she upgrades her apartment, her furniture is suddenly no longer nice enough or the proper fit for the layout. She has to get new organizers and new decor, and the utilities for heating and cooling a larger place also become a factor. We most commonly see celebrities, lottery winners, or professional athletes succumb to lifestyle creep and lose their fortunes. They decide their roles or positions mean they deserve, or are expected, to elevate all aspects of their life. They make assumptions about what someone in their new position or role should look like or what they should have. We all say these people are fools, and this would never happen to us, but the majority of us have been affected by some amount of lifestyle creep. Another common phrase for this behavior is "keeping up with the Joneses."

For you, it may be an increase in how many times you eat out in a month or getting the newest iPhone when your old phone was working perfectly fine. Maybe it was the expensive pairs of shoes you justified. Maybe it's all those monthly subscriptions, ones that, on their own, were probably okay, but when you add them all up, you realize it's a *lot* more than you thought.

No one is immune. For me, one such occasion was when I bought a pair of Frye boots. I bought them for about $400, and

I was so excited. I wore them a few times, and the bottom strap clasp kept opening. I took them back to the store, and they told me that they don't accept returns, and I would just need to pay for them to be repaired. I was floored! I had spent $400 on brand new boots, and I had to take them to have them repaired after wearing them twice! Well, that just pissed me off, and instead of taking them to the cobbler, I just cut the bottom strap off. Unfortunately, without the strap, I kept getting blisters, so I had to buy thicker socks to wear with them and little pad inserts to place around my ankles. Then winter came, and I realized I needed to waterproof the boots. The next year, I had to have them resoled. The *second* time I had those boots resoled I was also reading *The Millionaire Next Door*, by Thomas J. Stanley, which details how millionaires spend their money. As it turns out, the majority of millionaires spend less than $399 on their most expensive item of clothing. That information showed me I had no business paying $400 for boots if I ever wanted to get ahead in life. After all, it's the money you keep that makes you wealthy.

    Lifestyle creep is one of the biggest detriments to becoming wealthy or finding financial freedom. A lot of times it sneaks up on you. You'll have a good week, and instead of saving it, you may go shopping for the latest fashion or buy new furnishings. One of the challenging aspects of being a SIP is that you witness the spending habits of people with very high incomes (or people who are secretly in debt) on a daily basis when they come to your establishment, and it shifts your perception of how you could be spending.

    Hustlers are comfortable with money, which is not to say that they make the best decisions with it; there is a difference. You are constantly running numbers and scenarios, and that makes you better than most at doing back-of-the-envelope math. This is the same skill someone would develop if they were doing constant deal analysis. Whether you give yourself the credit for it or not, you are consistently managing the company's finances. Regardless of if you are managing a cash drawer or ringing up sales on a POS, you are serving as the catalyst for the transaction. You are good with other people's money, and it's time to translate that skill into working for you.

Hustle is an attitude, an identity, and an energy that can be used to create margin (the difference between what you make and what you spend). It can be helpful when you are first starting out, when you are trying to get to the finish line of a goal, and when you're working to adopt a positive money mindset. It is exactly that mindset that is necessary for someone who wants to achieve financial freedom, and you already have a lot of it. You are the epitome of a hustler, and once you get your money moving in the right directions, you will be unstoppable.

Financial Freedom Road Map Steps

Take these mindful action steps to explore and optimize your hustle, so you can continue moving yourself closer to financial freedom!

- Identify examples of hustle opportunities within your establishment—things you have done or things you have seen coworkers do. Make a list of all the ideas, pick a different idea each shift, and rotate them to keep things fresh.
- If your current job is limiting you or your income opportunities by not allowing you to fully hustle during a shift, begin looking for a new or secondary place of employment. If you were looking for a sign, this is it.

— Chapter Four —

Budget Like No One Is Watching (Because No One Is Watching)

A budget only has one rule: Do not go over budget.
Leslie Tayne

The past three chapters focused mostly on where you are, what you have to work with, and how that is different from most. In this chapter, we will talk about the framework for your budget with a large emphasis on the spending half of the equation. I know what you must be thinking: *Hell yeah!!!! Budgeting!!! Let's fucking DO this!!!* Okay, fine. I realize you probably aren't thinking that, but we need the understanding that budgeting provides in order to do the work needed to become financially free. Some of the work is mindset work—changing how we see or frame things—and some of the work is in setting up systems and boundaries.

As we discussed in Chapter 1, there are systemic issues and other larger things beyond our control that are working against SIPs, and while bigger conversations need to be had (at the corporate, state, and federal levels), there is something to be said for controlling what *you* can control and making the best with what you have, and that's what we will focus on in this chapter. We aren't going to go into this chapter with shame; we aren't going to judge our past selves; we aren't going to be dogmatic about spending. We will stay curious, we will question our assumptions, and we will experiment with our spending to find areas with the least amount of tension around them.

You've Been a Naughty, Naughty Spender

I worked in the fetish space for a number of years. It was a wonderfully supportive and inclusive community made up of individuals who know how to explore the depths of who they are and what they want. While not everything about the fetish world is applicable, I learned four key lessons that perfectly address budgeting. I promise we won't get too freaky.

Lesson #1: Only people who are into feet want to talk about feet, so *find your people*. If you are serious about budgeting and personal finance, it will be helpful to find a few like-minded people who you can talk to about your new and exciting endeavor. It makes all the difference if you find people you can connect with who are also just starting down this path. Studies show making changes with others who are doing the same leads to greater commitment and higher success.

Lesson #2: *The things you want most should be a part of your budget.* One of the things you learn in fetish work is that people like a lot of different things, and there is a broad range of things you can want. Your budget does not need to have the same line items as anyone else's. Everyone is unique, and it's okay to want, and budget for, the things you want. The caveat to that is just because you want all new clothes, a five-star vacation, or that brand new car doesn't mean you need it. But, if it is genuinely most important to you, get nuts with it, but keep your big picture in mind. It's important to remember that if you end up taking something out of your budget, you can always add it back later. Time spent without something gives us an opportunity to analyze its importance.

Lesson #3: *Boundaries are important, and it is your responsibility to communicate them.* If you are feeling pressured to spend money on things you don't want or need, it's important to communicate your boundaries. "No" is the new "yes." "Yes" is how others get what they want. Learning to navigate boundaries and saying *no* is necessary to get the things *you* truly want.

Lesson #4: *Discretion is encouraged.* There is no need to disclose anything about your budget or your finances. It's possible that no one in your group of friends or your family will be happy about your budget or savings goals, especially if they feel that you sticking to a budget will mean you are less likely to spend money on them or time with them. Your budget, like a fetish, can be your little secret. You don't need to share your goals or your budget numbers with others, especially if you are worried about being shamed or judged. No one needs to watch you budget, unless, of course, you are into that sort of thing…

As with all things relating to personal finance, feeling shame about the things you want will simply push you further away from budgeting. Budgeting is ultimately about supporting you as you discover what you want most in your one precious life and mapping out how you can get it. Budgeting is not making a list of the things you *think* you should want. You don't need to be an entirely different person to budget. You and your life are perfect, so start budgeting right where you are.

But I Don't **Want** *to Budget…*

Before we bust out the spreadsheets and notebooks, I want you to understand *why* all of this is necessary. Guess what? No one *wants* to budget. Everyone wants to spend money frivolously without a care in the world. I've worked on budgets with heiresses and multimillionaires, so I can tell you that even the extremely wealthy budget. Alas, as you know, SIPs live in a tough world where none of us have bottomless trust funds. It's even more important for us, so here we are.

You opened this book because you knew there was something more to be had, and this right here, your budget (aka your spending plan), is the agent of change that will get you to that "more." You spend the majority of your waking hours working for money. You collect it, you count it, and you straighten it. You take such good care to get it, only to have no idea where it all goes and why there is never anything left. Ask yourself why you focus so hard on one side of the equation (making the money), only to totally neglect the other side (managing it). Imagine being the best server but only for the first half of a guest experience. There you are, nailing the greeting of a guest yet ignoring them once you take their drink order. In short, it won't end well. Similarly, you need both earnings *and* strong money management to improve your financial life, not just one of the two. While money certainly isn't everything in life, nor should it be, considering you spend so much time chasing after it, don't you think you should spend at least a few minutes a week monitoring it to make sure it goes exactly where you want it to go?

If you are saying to yourself, "I know where it goes. It all goes to bills and groceries," then I challenge you to consider someone you know who makes less than you do. You can always find examples of people who earn less, and if we look closely, they can teach us some valuable lessons about our own spending. It's important for us to understand that financial freedom is achieved through accumulating wealth, and wealth is created by finding the difference between your income and your spending.

If you are someone who has ever impulsively bought a pair of shoes or has weekly nights out, then you are the perfect candidate for a budget. Impulse buying, whether it's shopping, eating, or drinking is your brain's way of trying to get a dopamine hit. Your brain is great at helping you get the thing it wants now, but it's not great at helping you plan for your future. Your brain loves immediate gratification.

Don't beat yourself up for your past purchases, but we will use those examples to find areas where you can create room in your budget to put funds elsewhere (we'll discuss further in later chapters), and we do that by analyzing our spending. You may be saying, "Barbara, just a few paragraphs ago you were telling me I could have whatever I want, and now you are coming for my shoes!" and yes, in a way, I am. While I do believe you can have whatever you want most, it's important to realize life is about choices, and we need to make tradeoffs to incorporate new and bigger goals.

Think back to Chapter 2, when we learned there are ways our environment works against us. The SIP environment can lead us to spend in excess, but if we stay honest with ourselves and make sure our decisions are guided by *our* goals—not made by the expectations of our environment or our peers—we can overcome those influences and spend less in areas that don't align.

I can't say it enough. You are a badass. You already have the hustle and skills required to excel at budgeting. If you can keep track of all your guests and the things they want, you can *crush* budgeting. All you need to be good with budgeting is tracking and adapting, two things that you already know how to do. You just need to try them out in a new setting (budgeting), and I'm going to help you.

Budgeting 101

Let's start at the beginning. A budget is an estimate of the income and expenses listed over a given time period; it's a goal of what you want the month to look like. Another way you can think of it is like a road map. The ultimate goal of a budget is to support your current life and to find and carve out money you can send to savings and invest to support your big and long-term goals. A lot of people work off a monthly budget, and virtually all business owners and entrepreneurs have a monthly budget. Like you, most businesses never have the same two months of income, and they rely on budgeting, guessing, and reworking their numbers to afford their expenses. A budget is the cornerstone to good financial planning, it's the most important piece to being good with your money, and it's the pièce de résistance and starting point for creating your path to financial freedom. Budgeting month after month will make you more comfortable with the process, and you will start to "know your numbers" soon enough. Once you know your numbers, you can start to examine where shifts can be made.

Following a budget involves a four-step process:

- **Step 1: Actuals.** Actuals is just a fancy word to describe the real (or actual) numbers for your spending. When you list and analyze your actuals, you are asking and answering a series of questions. *What are the elements of my current financial life? How much do I make now? Where does my money go each month? What does my money look like when I put it into categories and add those categories up? How do I feel when I see the numbers in the various categories? Do my numbers match my values?*
- **Step 2: Targets.** Targets are our goals. When you set targets, you are asking yourself those gut life questions. *What do I want out of life? What are my values? What are the things I like about my life now? What are the things I want out of my future? What do I want my life to look like in 10, 20, or even 40 years? Do I even know what I want?* Even if you have no clue what you want, don't worry; there is still a plan. Identify what your targets and goals are, even if they are vague, and compile them into a list.
- **Step 3: Forecast.** In forecasting, you take the targets, figure out what they cost, and map out how you can fit them into your new actuals. How do I reverse engineer my vision for my life? How much will the life I want cost? What do my goals look like financially? How long do I want these goals to take? Where am I willing to be flexible? What am I willing to sacrifice to achieve my goals? Identify the cost of your targets and break that price into smaller "payments" you can make over time.

   Example: One of your targets is to have a $10,000 emergency fund in your savings account. First, compare what is coming in to what is going out, and see how much you have left. Let's say you make $5,000 a month, and you spend $4,700 a month. That leaves $300. Dividing $10,000 by $300 is 33 months, or two *years and eight months. Does that work for you? If so, great! If not, head back to your actuals, and see where you can save money, so you are able to contribute more to your target each month.*

- **Step 4: Implement and Iterate.** Take action, plug your new numbers into a budget that you can adhere to, set up any accompanying accounts or systems, and adjust over time as you get new information. Track your spending (actuals), and make sure it aligns with your budget (targets) each month, once all the expenses have been posted and categorized.

Spending Time on Your Spending

The first step in creating a budget is getting a handle on your actuals—what you're actually spending. So, let's talk about how to track your money to make sure you have visibility with both your earnings and your spending. We have a tendency to lie to ourselves, so tracking is necessary to keep us honest and keep us on the path toward our goals.

To start strategizing your finances and putting together a budget, most personal finance advisors would have you start by adding up your income. However, unless you are someone who already diligently tracks your tips, you may have no idea what your total income is. For SIPs, we will need to start by looking at our spending. If we are currently spending most or all of our income, then looking at our spending will give us a pretty good idea of what our income is. Analyzing our spending is what will help us build out our budget and our strategy.

Maybe your current financial strategy is one where you work five shifts and make $120 per shift, cover your expenses, and everything leftover is for spending. Maybe your plan is to work seven days a week (including doubles) in the beginning of the month and offload shifts once you have expenses covered. Even if you think you don't have a plan, just remind yourself that you somehow manage your life every year, and within that lies some sort of a plan; unfortunately, it may not be the best plan if it's not serving *you*. Maybe you are behind on bills, and you feel as though you can't plan for the future because you can't even pay for the past. Well, I am here to tell you there is a system for everyone. You've heard the expression, "What's measured improves." It's time to start measuring your finances.

You need a plan. Yes, it takes dedication to execute a fixed expense budget on a fluctuating income and repeat the process each month (another reason why so many people just wing it, panic, and rely on credit). Luckily, there are *so* many ways to create a budget or spending plan, and not all of them involve writing down every transaction and saving all your receipts.

The Three Categories of Spending

First things first. Let's discuss how we will categorize your spending as this will be the basis for building your budget. All spending falls into three easy buckets: essential, lifestyle, and future. Remember, you are just looking at things, not judging and not changing anything—just looking.

1. **Essential** spending is anything you spend to make sure you can stay alive and stay safe. This includes:
   - Housing (the roof over your head)
   - Utility bills (gas, electric, water)
   - Medications
   - Cell phone bill (essential in today's world; it can keep you safe)
   - Groceries

The reason we keep essentials as a category is we need to know how low we can go. If shit goes down—we all are a little familiar with what this looks like—this is what we need simply to live. This category is also helpful as it allows us to mentally frame how much of our spending is not essential and how much choice we actually have.

2. **Lifestyle** spending is anything you *could* cut in the event of an emergency. If it doesn't keep you safe and alive, it falls into this category. This includes:
    - Streaming services
    - Fast food or to-go beverages
    - Dining out
    - Alcohol
    - Tobacco/recreational drugs
    - Gym membership
    - Travel
    - Monthly subscriptions
    - Clothing
    - Beauty services
    - Gifts and charity
    - Daycare
    - Car payment

You may be disputing some of my examples here, but the fact of the matter is, if shit went down, the person collecting your car payment would not be at the top of your hierarchy of needs.

3. **Future** spending is anything that helps Future You:
    - Paying down debt
    - Saving for future goals (down payment on a home or money in your emergency fund)
    - Investing for your future self (aka, retirement)

This is an important category. Even if you don't have anything to list under this column yet, it's important to list it anyway, acknowledge that it needs to be a part of your budget, and recognize you will be allocating future dollars here.

In summary, the essential category is helpful because it shows us how low our spending can get should we need to pull back to the bare minimum. The other two categories are not only vital to financial freedom, but they are also the pillars to creating a well-balanced life. The lifestyle category means you are including choice into your life. It also means you aren't living too frugally, and you are enjoying some of the here and now. The future category means you are including security into your life. You aren't just clouded by short-term thinking, robbing Future You of a quality life by only thinking about what you currently want. We need all three categories of spending to live financially free.

Build in Buffers

Now that we know the three buckets our money goes into, we need to address the fact that our monthly spending won't always look the same. Sometimes, it's helpful to make an additional note on our budget that identifies whether each expense is the same each month or whether it varies.

Fixed expenses are those that stay the same every month, such as rent. **Non-fixed or variable** expenses are those you anticipate but vary in cost or frequency. For example, your gas bill comes every month, but maybe it is much lower in summer months when your gas furnace isn't running. It's helpful to know which of your expenses are variable and what the range is, so you can build in a buffer. Keep in mind that lifestyle expenses can be either fixed or variable, as with monthly subscriptions (fixed) or takeout food (variable).

There are a few ways to build in a buffer. You could pad the account where the expenses are deducted. This would mean you deposit a fixed amount up front into the account every year or season that would cover the fluctuations. Another way to build in buffers is to round up your budget number each month to cover the difference of the highest cost within the range.

> *Example: My electric bill averages $100 per month in the winter and $200 in the summer because of my air conditioning. Padding the account would mean I budget for $100 per month, but I preload the account with $600 extra to cover the fluctuations of the summer months. Rounding up would mean I budget for $150*

a month during the winter so that by the time I get to summer, there is enough in the account to cover the additional charges.

If you have large fluctuations or seasonal income, then padding makes sense; if not, then rounding would probably work better.

The Cost of Living

Since many of us have been flying by the seat of our pants, actually writing out all of your expenses can come with some sticker shock. Alas, the only way to get over it is to go through it. Grab a piece of paper or open up an Excel spreadsheet, pour yourself a glass of wine, and buckle up. Start by listing all your monthly fixed expenses. If you know what an item costs, such as your rent, write it out. But, don't get bogged down in the specifics yet. Focus on getting the name of the expense written out (groceries, daycare, rent, etc.), and once you have them all listed, *then* you can go back and figure out the cost of each.

To be clear, this task is not exciting. It is not sexy. Frankly, it sucks. Stick with it! The cure for boredom is curiosity; your money is exciting stuff, so stay curious about it! After you come up with all of your fixed monthly costs, then list all of your non-fixed or variable monthly costs. With variable costs, it might be helpful to add subcategories, but make sure to use ones that work best for you.

Example: Bars, restaurants, and fast food are three common and different budget subcategories, which confuses me. Where are you supposed to put Taco Bell Cantina? Instead, I put expenses for bars, restaurants, and fast food all together into "dining out" and set a monthly budget amount for the entire "dining out" subcategory. If you, on the other hand, are trying to cut down on fast food, you may want to keep that subcategory separate, so you can keep an eye on how much you are spending there. Another example is how you might decide to include coffee shop visits in the "dining out" category, or if you are trying to manage your latte spending, you could use "coffee" as a separate subcategory as well.

Now, you may be thinking, *How the eff am I supposed to know how much I spend on tacos every month?* That's a valid point. If you want, here is where you can pull out bank statements if you have them, but if you don't, then you will have to guess on your spending categories (and subcategories) and on the amount. I think guessing is more fun because later, when you are actually tracking, you can see how off your assumptions were and what categories you may have missed. It's up to you, but at this point, don't feel slowed down by looking at your statements. For now, just keep going and try to add all of those other once-a-month, once-a-year, or once-off expenses. Other examples of categories are beauty products, beauty services, entertainment, pharmacy, clothing, gifting, home decor, and travel.

Once you've listed all of the recurring spending categories, do the following:

1. Fill in the monthly cost next to the expense name.
2. Write the spend category next to the expense cost: essential, lifestyle, or future.
3. Add up all the expenses in each spend category. What is the monthly spend total for lifestyle, essentials, and future?
4. Add the three categories together to get your monthly spending amount.
5. Divide each individual category total into the amount of your total monthly spending to get the percentage number for each category of spending.
6. If you included subcategories, take a look at those totals separately and see how you feel about them. Were you surprised, angry, or embarrassed by them? Did the

numbers feel in line with how you would value them? Whatever you are feeling, make a note. It may help you when you explore making shifts in your spending.

Example: If your total monthly spending is $5,500, and you spent $2,700 on essential spending, $3,100 on lifestyle spending, and $0 on future spending, you would divide $2,700 by $5,500, which would mean you spend 44 percent on essential spending. Doing the same for lifestyle and future, you'd see 56 percent of your spending is on lifestyle items, and 0 percent is on the future.

Once you have one month of spending written out, everything categorized, and the percentage of spending calculated, congratulations! You're practically an expert! Keep going! Get a few more months under your belt. You can do this by going backward if you have good records, or you can simply continue the process each month. Having a few months of spending listed and categorized does two critical things. First, it helps you better understand your spending habits, and second, it helps give you a base for what your annual income may be. To find this, take the average of your spending for three months (add the three months together and divide by three), and multiply that by 12. Keep in mind that most SIPs have some seasonality to their income, but pay attention to how that number makes you feel! Moving forward, you will track your tips, which means you must *write down everything you make, including cash tips*. That is the only way to get an accurate picture of your income.

As you start to get a handle on your averages and percentages, you can then start to make bigger plans and allocate funds toward goals. Averages are what matter because there will always, *always* be things that cause our living expenses to fluctuate. We will never deal with absolutes, and no two months will ever be the same, which is why it's even more important to know our numbers on the spend side. With that, we can create our limits and our guides.

The Three-Category Budget

Knowing what you spend each month is only so helpful. What you really need to know is how your spending stacks up and how it can be improved. That is where the three-category budget, also referred to as the 50-30-20 rule, comes in handy.

The three-category budget is a budgeting guideline that advises you to spend 50 percent of your income on essentials, 30 percent on lifestyle, and 20 percent on future (savings, debt payoff, and investments). This 50-30-20 budgeting system has long been prescribed by financial advisors and experts. I prefer to call it a three-category budget because not everyone can (or should) use the same percentages. That being said, the three-category budget is the budgeting strategy that we will stick with for the remainder of the book and also the strategy that mirrors the three categories of spending (essentials, lifestyle, and future) that we already talked about, which is the basis of building our budget. I like the three-category budget best because it doesn't require you to go too deep down the budgeting rabbit hole, but it allows you to keep an eye on the overall picture.

> ### *Tip for the Tipped*
>
> *It's important to note that you can adjust your three-category budget percentages to numbers that better fit your goals and lifestyle. You may find 50-30-20 isn't feasible for you, especially if you live in a higher cost-of-living area, such as New York. You may need to adjust your numbers slightly to something like 60-20-20. However, if one of your categories falls below 10 percent, it could mean that you have either a spending problem or an income problem.*

If your categories don't look like 50-30-20 (from our example budget, maybe more like 44-56-0), don't worry, we are just getting started, and there is plenty of time to make adjustments. Let's look at a few ways you can shift these numbers if needed.

Balancing Your Spending

If your current essential category spend is more than 50 percent of your total spending, the first thing to do is check to make sure all those expenses are required for your life and safety. If you determine they are, there are two main ways to get your number closer to 50: make more money or tackle your big three.

Make more money. I say this lightly knowing this cannot be fixed with the wave of a wand, but the truth is, if you are spending, for example, 70 percent of your income on essentials, and nothing can come down in terms of cost, you need to find a way to make more. Instead of listing all of the reasons you think you cannot make more money, approach this with a question. "If I had to, how could I make more money?" The answer may come the longer you sit with the question.

Tackle your big three. If it's not an income problem, and your essentials number is bigger than 50, then you may be spending too much on the big three: **housing, transportation, and food**. The big three are the fastest way to change your overall budget and your financial life. If you cut down on those three expenses, you can change the course of your entire future. Here are a few rules of thumb when looking at the numbers around your big three. Keep in mind that rules of thumb are guidelines or principles that are thought of as "roughly accurate" and can therefore apply to many. They are a great place to start, but don't feel like you need to stick with them for life.

1. **Rent or mortgage** is generally suggested to be no more than 25 percent of your total monthly spend (or 50 percent of your essential category). Housing is crazy expensive these days, so if you find yourself over that percentage, look for ways to get that number down. Getting a smaller place or a roommate can help cut costs.

In that same vein, house hacking—buying or renting a home and having housemates who help you pay the rent or mortgage—is a great way to get ahead financially, and it doesn't need to be forever.
2. **Check your transportation costs.** Transportation (car payment, insurance, gas, etc.) is suggested to be no more than 15 percent of your total monthly spend. If it's higher, consider downgrading to a cheaper car, or find ways to save on gas. Consider walking, biking, or using public transportation for outings and errands. Include other SIPs in saving money by carpooling.
3. **Watch your grocery bill.** Food should account for roughly 10 percent of your total monthly spend (or 20 percent of your essential category). Grocery shopping tip: Never go grocery shopping when you are tipsy, hungry, or pissed. You'll thank me later.

Though moving out of your home or trading in a new car for a used car may seem dramatic, and you may feel you are losing out on some of the initial upfront costs, these are actual ways you can put yourself first and on a faster path toward financial freedom.

Landing a Budget

Once you know what you are actually spending on the essential, lifestyle, and future categories, adjust your budget numbers and set target goals, but be sure to be realistic. If groceries have cost you $500 every month for the past three months, don't list it as $400 unless you have specific ideas to save on groceries while staying healthy and safe.

When I first started budgeting, I read one guideline that said by 30 years of age, you should aim to have $47,000 invested toward retirement, or one full year of income. That made me sit up straight. I definitely did not have that in savings at 30 years old. I realized I wasn't allocating enough toward Future Me, and Future Me was likely going to have a bad back from my years of working in heels. She was going to want to sit in a nice hot tub and take quality vacations. The more I started to think about Future Me, the more I started to prioritize her and budget for her.

One way you can jumpstart your commitment to saving for Future You is to write out or visualize your perfect day. Assume you are retired or maybe even working part-time. How are you spending your perfect day not working? What gets you out of bed in the morning? What do you enjoy doing each day? Where do you live? What is it like there? What do you wear? What do you eat? Consider things such as how much you need to live on in a year of retirement (post tax).

This mental exercise is how I came to realize that retired me will need a hot tub surrounded by trees. I don't have everything figured out yet; for instance, I don't know where that hot tub will live or what type of trees will be there, but I know that I want to be able to enjoy unlimited fruit and seltzers.

After you create your budget and have a clear idea of your spending, you will need to set up a system (which can include a combination of different tactics) to monitor the numbers and help you stay within the three-category goals. For starters, we know your system will include tracking your income and spending every month and checking your spending against your budget. If needed, you will adjust your numbers and try to stay aligned with your spending category targets.

One tactic for following a budget like this—and a very easy way if you are a mostly or all-cash earner—is the envelope system. I imagine you may be familiar with this. Essentially, you put your money (in cash) into envelopes that match the expense lines on your budget—then you spend solely from those envelopes. Once an envelope runs out, you cannot spend any more on that expense or subcategory for the month. Even though it feels low tech, it's one of the most effective and highly recommended strategies for staying on a budget, even for non-cash earners.

The upside to the envelope system is that it works well for all cash earners, for people who need tactile ways to organize, and for those with poor or no credit. Also, there is something about using cash that makes it harder to part with than simply swiping your debit card. In fact, one strategy suggested for nine-to-fivers who end up in debt is to switch to using only cash because it's easier to track and emotionally harder to spend.

Here's how to put the envelope system into action:

1. Buy a box of envelopes.
2. Write the name of each expense or subcategory (i.e., rent, electric, dining out, coffee, gas, etc.) on your envelope, along with the goal amount. Feel free to decorate your envelopes!

> **Tip for the Tipped**
>
> *When I was doing envelopes, I also created a shoebox piggy bank for a big savings goal, and I glued inspirational images all over it. I was so excited each time I put money into that box.*

3. Prioritize the envelopes based on importance. I suggest prioritizing savings, and we will explore why in the coming chapters.
4. As money comes in, distribute it among the envelopes, either using your priority system or breaking up each "deposit" by percentages.
5. Take money out of your allocated envelopes whenever you need to pay a bill or want to spend.

As with anything, the envelope system isn't perfect. The downside is that cash allows for easy access for impulse spenders, doesn't allow for any automation, doesn't allow for growth, is easy to forget when you leave the house, and is a major security risk, as it can be lost or stolen with no solid avenues for recovery.

> **Tip for the Tipped**
>
> If you use an envelope system or other cash management system, I recommend an in-home safe. Once your savings envelopes fill up, I recommend transferring that cash to a bank or a safety deposit box.

Excel at Excel

Another tactic for tracking your spend against a budget is a good ol' Excel spreadsheet, similar to the way you created your initial budget. It's a classic, no-frills way to see your numbers in a variety of ways. I like this because you can have a tab for each month of the year and can toggle between tabs for easy comparison. It's also great to look back and see how far you've come and see your changing spending habits.

It's low-tech in that you can import your transactions from your bank or credit cards, or you can simply manually enter them. If you have Google Drive, you can use Google Sheets. Using a spreadsheet app (both Google Drive and Excel come in app form) allows you to enter your transactions, especially your cash ones, on your phone as you spend and lets you analyze them on your computer. If you are less tech savvy, you can use a notebook. In the back of this book at Appendix 5, you will find a starter budget format, or you can use Google to find other examples.

Get Techy With It

Now let's talk about tech-based budgeting tools, which are another tactic for tracking your spend against your budget. Most people have heard of Mint, but YNAB and Qube are also popular budgeting apps. HomeBudget, Goodbudget, Mvelopes, and SimpleBudget, all allow for manual (cash) transactions if or when you aren't using a bank account. Whichever app you try, the interface should tell you how much you are spending monthly within the categories you use to tag your transactions. You can link your bank accounts, making apps a low time investment tactic (Yay!), but I also think this feature makes them easier to ignore. When left to their own algorithms, the apps will incorrectly categorize your spending, and you won't be able to clearly see your numbers. If you do go with one of these options, check your apps regularly to make sure your money is being categorized properly, and all of your accounts are syncing.

There are also apps for tracking only the income side of things. You can mix apps if you need, or you can use an app for tip tracking only. Remember, if you don't track your income along with your expenses, you will only have half the picture and will struggle with your budget. If you are new to budgeting, the apps may seem like a sexier option. In all honesty, though, I think creating your budget from scratch through Excel or a notepad does a better job of helping you. It forces those numbers to carve themselves into your brain, so you can make bigger and better long-term decisions.

The Anti-Budget

A more advanced method of tracking your spending is what I consider to be the graduation budget, or the anti-budget. The anti-budget is just that—not a budget. It's a spending system you set up that allows you not to have to track each individual expense. The idea behind it is to save first and spend the rest. There are a few things I recommend before you try this type of spending plan.

1. You should already have a pretty good understanding of your typical spending numbers.
2. You should have enough funds to create a healthy buffer in the spending account. Ideally, you would have enough saved in each account for a full months' worth of expenses before the month starts.
3. You should separate your fixed monthly expenses into one account and savings into another. Whatever is left

over should be directed into a third account for your flex or discretionary spending.

So, you'll have three accounts: one for bills (your essential category), one for discretionary spending (the lifestyle category), and one for savings (the future category).

The strategy of having three accounts, or "buckets," is that you direct your income into each of your separated spending accounts where your bills and obligations come out automatically. What is left in your discretionary account is what you are allowed to spend for the week or month.

This is a very advanced budgeting tactic, and I only recommend this if you have some savings you can use as buffers in each account *and* if you really know what your monthly spending is.

Know Your Numbers

Whether you get a journal, start an Excel spreadsheet, download an app, have a box of envelopes, or use a combination of any of these tactics, the most important part is actually including all your income and your expenses. You need to use your real numbers—no cheating yourself here. Budget as a boss would—after all, you are the real boss of your money and your life.

If you are like me, there were many years when I had no idea how much I made. I tailored my guess to whomever I was talking. Budgeting, and actually knowing what I made, gave me a sense of legitimacy and made me more accountable with my money. Once I knew how much I made, it became real, and I became committed to being a better steward of it. I couldn't ignore the fact I had no savings, nor could I pretend I was spending less than I actually was. The numbers were a cold splash of water to the face. Once I knew them, things started to change.

You need to know your own numbers as easily as you can recall the various numbers at your work, such as the costs of menu items, or table numbers. At work, knowing your numbers as you go through your shift helps you make short-term decisions, such as, "Have I made enough to get cut?" Knowing your numbers in life helps you make bigger decisions, such as, "Did I put enough away in savings this month to also be able to take a Friday off or to give myself two sick days?" It is critical to know where you are starting, so you can see where you are going and how you plan to get there. This is how you make the right decisions to avoid sacrificing your future plans.

There is no downside to budgeting and saving, only upsides. The more you budget, the more you will replace the very helpful rules of thumb with your own specific goals. You will become clearer on what you value and will enjoy spending more on exactly those things. The more intentional you are, and the more you live according to your own values and financial freedom plan, the better your life will get. Tracking and keeping a spending plan in place means you can create the big goals that will help get you to financial freedom.

Financial Freedom Road Map Steps

Take these mindful action steps to create your budget, so you can continue moving yourself closer to financial freedom!

- Create a budget:
    - List all your spending categories.
    - Track your expenses.
    - Try to stay under your budget numbers.
    - Make sure you have some money allocated toward savings.
    - Check out the monthly budget tracker in Appendix 5.
- Choose a tactic to track your spending, and try to stick with it for a month. If you mess up, start again, or try a different tracking tactic. It can take a few tries or different methods for it to stick. If you get burned out, take a break without going into full "fuck it" mode, and start again when you have more bandwidth.

- Track all your income, including all your cash tips. You need to know how much you make, so you can be sure to spend it exactly the way you want.
- Be a budget voyeur. Look at other people's budgets by Googling "How I spend my $30,000 a year (or insert your number here) budget." Does it look like what you thought it would? Were there expenses that surprised you?
- Write out your perfect day. Be specific—what you are eating, what you are wearing, where you are, who you are with, and what you are doing. This is what you are working toward!
- Get an accountability buddy, someone you feel comfortable reviewing your budget with. Plan to meet at regular or monthly intervals. If you can't find someone in your life, try joining a Facebook group.

— Chapter Five —
Pay Your Sexy Self First

If you prioritize yourself, you are going to save yourself.
Gabrielle Union

In Chapter 2, I mentioned having the experience of me spending what I had and others spending what they had *left over* after they had fulfilled obligations of bills, savings, and investing. At the time, I didn't include savings and investing in my money obligations. I recall people buying drinks or a round and later announcing they were tapped, and they either left, or someone else would kick in for the next round to keep the good times rolling. Looking back, the only time money was discussed was when it meant the end of someone's fun for the day.

Money is one of the only truly taboo topics left. If you ask 10 people to answer either how many times a week they have sex or the amount of money in their bank accounts, the majority of people would tell you how little sex they are having. SIPs are usually pretty comfortable talking about money (in addition to sex). They share with their peers how much they make in a shift and how much they pay in rent. Unfortunately, across the industry, the conversation hasn't shifted to the more mundane, yet critically important, topics such as how much money is saved every month, where it is kept, how, if at all, it's invested and with which platform. Do you have a strategy or allocation? If you test the waters by talking to your guests about this stuff, you will likely see them squirm in their seats as you begin to ask questions. Ask them what they invest in, and it's likely they will just say index or mutual funds, which, in short, means they don't really know; they are just doing what people in their HR departments told them to do, and that is paying themselves first.

I Got 99 Problems, But Paying Myself Ain't One

The concept of "paying yourself first" initially came from a book called *The Richest Man in Babylon*, by George S. Clason, which was written over a century ago. The book is set 4,000 years in the past and teaches amazing financial lessons through parables about a poor scribe who becomes the richest man in Babylon, simply by following the same basic financial principles we are discussing in this book. The most important concept taught is why paying yourself first is a must to achieve financial wealth. This once profound advice was shouted from the tops of the personal finance mountains, carved on tablets, and passed on to children at such a high frequency that it's either lost its impact or been buried in the things we don't say, so we don't sound like our parents. The thing is, it's great advice and really the only way to become financially free.

Answer this question: Who is more effective at collecting and hanging onto your money on a regular basis, you or the IRS? That question seems like a no-brainer—the IRS. They are experts at getting the money; they send notices, they have the power to levy and garnish your wages or accounts, and they even have the power to put those who evade taxes in prison. For many there is no greater fear than getting in the crosshairs of the IRS. You will always figure out a way to pay them… eventually. Now, let's look at the other side of that question, *you*. You tell yourself you should save, but after everyone else is paid, and there is no more money, are you sending yourself late notices or tallying what you should have saved last month and adding that to next month's savings goal? No! You likely forgive yourself and tell yourself you'll do better next month or the next big tip night, consistently putting it off to a day that will likely never come.

What if we change the question slightly: Who is more important, you or the IRS? Hopefully your answer changes, and you would say *you*. You are the most important, and you come first. That is why you need to pay yourself first. Always.

Treat Yo' Self!

In Chapter 4, we explored the three-category budget (the 50-30-20 rule). We know that 20 percent is divided between savings, investing, and debt paydown. The question is, how should you divide that 20 percent among those three categories? I generally say you should decide what is best for you when you break up that 20 Percent. After all, personal finance is personal, but my preference is that at least 10 percent of it should go toward Future You (savings and retirement).

> *Example: Let's say you have debt that you really want to pay off. In this case, maybe you allocate your 20 percent as follows: 10 percent to debt, five percent to retirement, and five percent to your emergency fund. When it comes down to you versus the IRS, this means that when you get any money—any money—10 percent (five percent to retirement plus five percent to savings) of that money immediately needs to go toward Future You, and 10 percent needs to go toward paying down debt before you pay anyone else, including the IRS.*

Think of prioritizing these funds as your personal tariff. Paying yourself first does not mean pay yourself *only* once you make sure you can cover rent or groceries; it means *always* first. Allocating 10 percent to your future self (retirement and savings combined) may seem like a lot at first, but let's say you made $100 working a day shift. Would you really notice a huge difference in your life if you only made $90? No! If you came up

$10 short on bills or taxes, you would do what you always do as a hustler, and you would pick up another few shifts, spend a little less on this or that, and figure out a way to pay the bills. You will always figure it out.

It is this slight shift in perspective, practice, and setting up your future financial system that will allow you to become financially free. It might not seem like enough to even be worth it, but let's say you work five day shifts a week, and you make $100 each shift. If you pay yourself first, then you will have collected $10 from each shift, which adds up to $50 a week. If you did this for the 52 weeks in a year, you would have set aside $2,520. Now, divide that $2,520 by $100 (what you would make in a shift), and voila! That is 25 fewer shifts Future You will need to work. Future You will thank you for that!

We tell ourselves a lot of lies. Lies are our brain's way of creating neat stories, so it can shut down with thinking and allow itself to rest. We say we can't save because we don't make enough, because we have too many expenses, or because we have to help take care of others. Even saying the words "pay yourself first" feels selfish. How can you save for Future You when current loved ones are struggling or have extremely pressing needs, or when you already feel your money is stretched to the max? Think about it from a health perspective. Imagine if you told your loved ones you needed to start taking a specific supplement, and by doing so, you'd be able to live 10 years longer. Your loved ones would want you to be able to set aside your money, so you could focus on getting healthier. Those who truly love and care about you will want you to be able to set up safety nets for your future.

Your money is no one's business but your own, and every person should have their own money. If you are someone who is experiencing financial abuse from a spouse or a loved one, then I am in favor of building a squirrel stash. We are talking about financial freedom, and that means you need to have control of and over your money. Paying yourself for your future is not selfish; it means you are being a good steward of your money. You are ensuring you will be okay as you age, and you can age without worrying about food and basic needs. Wanting to make sure Future You is not homeless or hungry is not a selfish desire. You cannot help others if your own basic needs are not met. If you feel supported, you may want to start talking about your money or retirement goals with your loved ones. In our house, we call our money talks "money dates."

Pay Yourself First Your Way

If you want to get creative with your own version of the 10 percent rule (or 20 percent if you don't have debt, or 30 percent or more if you want to retire early), you can find many fun ways to shape the "pay yourself first" strategy in the SIP industry. If you are a server or a bartender, you can select a specific table, section, or set of bar stools to be your dedicated "saving and investing" section. Take all the tips you get from the guests at table 22, and automatically put them into your investment account.

If you are a valet driver, you can select a type of car or color to dedicate to savings. If you are a dancer, dedicate a bill type or all proceeds from a specific song set or day of the week. As a hairstylist, perhaps you dedicate the tips from clients who tell terrible boyfriend stories to your savings and investing accounts. Having strategies or games like these will help you hold yourself accountable and will bring whimsy and fun to what otherwise (at least in the beginning) may be a difficult or woefully boring part of money management.

Shifting Your Mindset

Paying yourself first is all about shifting your mindset to include Future You into your current plans because let's face it, if you can't manage to save $10 out of every $100 for long-term goals or retirement *today*, then it's highly unlikely you'll ever be able to save $10,000 out of every $100,000 *later*, when Future You needs it the most. The long-term is coming whether we like it or not, and you need to be in the habit of paying Future You before you pay Current You. Current You is the only advocate that Future You has. There may not exist a right way, but what I do know is that not putting yourself first will always be wrong.

If you've seen the movie *Hustlers*, then you watched as the strippers spent hundreds of thousands of dollars on cars, outfits, nights out, and lavish apartments. They were living their best lives in the moment, but they weren't thinking of their future selves at all. Even though they were bringing in hundreds of thousands of dollars, they were not in the habit of paying themselves first or thinking of their futures, so they continued on as they had been—spending what they made and screwing over future them. If they had put even half of what they made, say $100,000, in an index fund in 2008 when the movie takes place, in just a little over ten years, it would have tripled. Now, that is maybe an extreme example, but we all know we have had times of abundance, and instead of making the best decisions and building good habits, we have pretended the money didn't enter our worlds, and we made a different choice, one where we didn't do anything for our future selves.

You may be telling yourself that you cannot pay yourself first because you have aggressive creditors calling you, and that weighs heavy on your thoughts. No worries; I've got you covered. If you have creditors calling, and your debt management strategy (more on this in Chapter 7) is not one where you can avoid creditors using things like levees and garnishments against you, then paying yourself will look a little different, but it is still possible! The first thing I suggest is checking your state's laws to see if creditors are prevented from going after your accounts. Google "can creditors go after my IRA in [state you live in]." If not, then it's good news! You can invest in an Individual Retirement Account, or IRA (more on this in Chapter 8). However, if your state *does* allow creditors to go after your bank and retirements accounts, then pay yourself first with cash and a safety deposit box until you can clear the creditors.

> **Reminder**
>
> *This is a slow burn. Paying yourself first does not mean you will wake up tomorrow and suddenly be rich. It's more than just a mental shift. If you commit and implement paying yourself first, then you will change your life. Say it loud and proud in the mirror before every shift: "I pay myself first."*

Tracking Your Net Worth

One of my favorite ways to track whether you really are paying yourself first (and making progress on your path to financial freedom) is by tracking your net worth. Your net worth is the value of your assets (things or money you own) minus your liabilities (things you owe).

How to calculate your net worth:

1. **Make a list of all your assets.** Assets include things such as how much cash you have, how much money you have in the bank, how much your house or car is worth, and any other items of value. There's no need to get too granular here; you can leave the gift cards and coin jars off the list for now (though my coin jars once got up to over $1,200 and I would totally put that on my spreadsheet).
2. **Make a list of the liabilities.** Liabilities are the things you owe. Don't list monthly living expenses here as those are expected every month and won't change your overall financial picture. Include things such as a mortgage, personal or student loans, credit card balances that you carry for more than one month, or your car loan.
3. **Subtract your liabilities from your assets.** The remainder is your net worth.

Don't be discouraged if it is lower than you thought it would be. If you are just now, for the first time, seeing you have a negative net worth (or just far less than imagined), repeat after me: "My net worth is not my self-worth." With time and consistency, you will grow your net worth and your personal finance skills.

I started out doing my net worth calculation monthly, and it helped me see that budgeting and paying myself first was really working. Now, I typically do my net worth calculation yearly or every six months, and I get so excited to see the numbers make bigger jumps. Every time I calculate my net worth, I create a new tab in my Excel sheet and name the page with the date, so I can see how far I've come.

Once you start regularly calculating and tracking your net worth and start seeing the numbers shift in the right direction, you'll understand why paying yourself first is considered the first rule of personal finance and the Golden Rule for all financial advisors and money managers. It is this nonnegotiable, "I will save and invest first" mentality, combined with your hustler attitude, that will get you to financial freedom.

Financial Freedom Road Map Steps

Take these mindful action steps to start paying yourself first, so you continue moving yourself closer to financial freedom!

- Start a net worth tracking spreadsheet, and create a new tab for each month to compare. You can find a net worth tracker example in Appendix 6.
- If you have debt, review your state's laws regarding creditors and what accounts they can access.
- Start getting in the mindset that 20 percent of what you make every shift is for Future You (through savings, investing, and debt reduction).

— Chapter Six —

In Case of Fire (or Getting Fired), Break Glass

The question isn't who is going to let me; it's who is going to stop me.
Ayn Rand

I'd never had or heard of an emergency fund until I was 33 years old, and this was after I had been helping some of my friends and coworkers with their money and budgets. My wife was working for a small startup that had been bought out by an insurance company. Their initial product was an app dedicated to teaching women about investing, and her benefit package included working with an assigned financial advisor. Having assumed I'd never get the chance to work with a financial advisor, I jumped at the idea of having one for free.

I remember getting on the call with our advisor, Jeff. He asked us a bunch of questions, pushed the idea of needing many types of insurance, avoided most of our questions about investments, and said he would forward our plan in a few weeks. I was furious. It felt like a sales call, and on top of that, he said the first thing we needed to worry about was getting an emergency fund. He said this was an account that held funds totaling six months of expenses that you would never invest but that would just sit in a savings account. I was aghast! We lived in New York at the time, a place where everything is ridiculously expensive. On average, we were spending over $6,000 a month. I did the math and realized he wanted us to save almost $36,000, not for a house, not for a vacation, but just to sit there! I wrote off his suggestion immediately. He was in a very different situation than I was. He made finance income (straight, white, male, finance income). He lived in Texas where expenses were much lower. He was probably older. He probably got money from his family. Finally, I told myself that only he was doing this and that he was an outsider as no one else I knew had this… Or so I thought.

Our "plan" came two weeks later, but in the interim, that financial advisor had angered me with advice that felt all wrong. It ignited a flame in me, and I set out to prove him wrong. I started listening to two podcasts, one called *Afford Anything* and the other called *So Money*. Within a few episodes of both, I heard the hosts, Paula and Farnoosh, and many of their listeners who called in talk about their own emergency funds. Some of the callers were people with similar or worse life circumstances, and they were creating emergency funds. I couldn't deny it. Jeff the financial advisor was right—about this one thing—much to my fury.

Lucky for you, I've learned to channel my fury into something more productive. In this chapter, we will talk about the emergency fund. An emergency fund is a way to protect both current us and future us from outside forces; in other words, an emergency fund lets us be masters of our own destiny. We will walk through the ways to think about an emergency fund and discuss why we need them, how much an emergency fund should have, where to keep it, and what exactly to use it for.

What is an Emergency Fund?

Maybe, like me, you didn't know what an emergency fund was or what it should be. Maybe you are telling yourself you have a few hundred or a few thousand dollars stashed away, and that is your emergency fund. You may be thinking you still have a few hundred dollars available on one or two credit cards, and you are considering that to be an emergency plan.

Well, let's start by defining what an emergency fund is. An emergency fund is a separate account or safe where you keep liquid, ready-to-access money (aka, cash or a bank account). We will get into credit cards in the next chapter, but for now, understand an emergency fund cannot be a credit card.

The purpose of an emergency fund is to provide you with easy-to-access money that you can use in the event of an emergency. I have found there are two main purposes for an emergency fund. The first reason you'd need an emergency fund is for those "oh, fuck" emergencies, such as unexpected car troubles, medical bills, or emergency pet surgeries. The second reason is for the times when you really just need a way to say, "Fuck you," in a tough situation. We will dive into the "fuck you" part of your emergency fund later, but simply put, these are funds to cover the sudden loss of a job.

Oh Fuck!

So how much do you need in your emergency fund? There are a lot of ways to calculate an emergency fund, but what's interesting is that in all of my research in trying to prove Jeff and the emergency fund concept wrong, I didn't see anyone saying that less was better, and the generally agreed upon six months of expenses, give or take a few depending on your own circumstances, has been going strong for decades. If you fell out of your chair, then you are having the exact same reaction I did when this was explained to me.

If you are just starting to pay yourself first, then you may just have one account called "savings," but as we learned in Chapter 4, when paying yourself first, you need to be as specific as possible when allocating money toward savings and investing. This may mean you have more than one savings account. The good news is that your emergency fund *is* part of the savings portion of your budget (part of that 20 percent in the 50-30-20 strategy) that we've been talking about.

> **Reminder**
>
> *The 20 percent for future is any combination of both savings and investing that makes sense for your long-term (like your emergency fund) and retirement goals.*

Now that you know what an emergency fund is, it's time to get specific and set up the goal (what emergencies it can be used for and how much we want the finished amount to be) and decide how to execute the transaction (where it's going and how it's getting there).

Funding Your "Oh Fuck!" Emergency Fund

Saving money is hard, but as with anything else, it is a habit and a muscle that requires practice to maintain. Therefore, while financial advisors will say six months of your expenses, I suggest you start with three because the best goal is the one you attain. Once you hit three months' worth of savings, throw yourself a little party! After that, you can work toward the next three months.

There are a lot of life hacks to help you achieve your goals. Are you into vision boards? Making check lists, goal thermometers, or using motivation apps? Maybe it is finding accountability buddies or creating accountability social media posts. I'm here for all of it. I am willing to try whatever has worked for other people, both the work and the "woo woo," and I think you need both sometimes.

When my spouse, Casey, and I decided to set up an emergency fund, we chose for all our other goals to take a backseat. We took the goal for our emergency fund (six months of expenses) and divided it by 24 months. We thought two years sounded like a reasonable amount of time to make some serious sacrifices without getting too cranky. Amazingly, it only took Casey and I a year and a half to save our emergency fund, and we celebrated with a little money dance every few months when we hit our goals.

Cut Out Unnecessary Spending

To start tackling your own emergency fund, try cutting out unnecessary spending. Starting this way will mean you can grow your savings in little ways here and there, without feeling as if you are cutting too far back. Cutting down, for you, may mean only going out to eat once a month instead of once every week. Maybe it's putting things in that online shopping cart but stopping short of actually ordering them. I managed to cut out $200 of spending *per week*, which I kept up for 18 months and saved $36,000.

> *Reminder*
>
> *Everyone has unnecessary spending; if you can't seem to figure out what your unnecessary spending is, look to that someone you know who makes less than you. What are they spending money on? What aren't they spending money on?*

Get creative. For example, if you wanted to focus on cutting down on clothing purchases, do a no-spend challenge. There are many ways to freshen up old costumes or fashion. If you have a light-colored outfit, buy a box of dye and go darker, or you can try layering or adding removable or fixed accessories. Swapping fashion with industry peers, if hygienic (currently, RentTheGString.com does not exist), can also expand your wardrobe. Get your shoes resoled. Did you see something great online or at a thrift store, but it isn't your size? Sometimes it's still cheaper to buy it and have it tailored than it is to buy brand new. Fashion is a depreciating asset, especially with trendy items. Focus on items that will stand the test of time that don't exceed your spending plan and are versatile.

There were many other things we did to achieve our emergency fund goal amount. We cut out a lot of our eating out, drinks with friends, travel, fashion, beauty expenses, and the gym. We prepped our meals at home. What we realized was that most of the time, we had been the ones suggesting going out when others were perfectly fine staying in or being low-key. We realized we would pay for other's drinks or traveling costs to see friends and family because we had somehow convinced ourselves the other people in our lives didn't have as much freedom as we did (due to children, job flexibility, etc.) and that we should pay to accommodate other people without first choosing to fund our own goals. It wasn't our friends' and families' fault. If we had said to them, "Actually, we are putting off eating out while we save up some money and get ourselves out of debt," I guarantee most of our loved ones would have been incredibly supportive.

Hustle and [Make That Cash] Flow

I get it; it doesn't sound fun to cut out all the frills, and I'm not suggesting you remove all joy from your life—far from it. The truth is, there are tons of ways to budget, cut down spending, and still find great deals that allow you to splurge occasionally. Whether you aren't quite willing to give up your daily pastry fund, or your margins are still too slim, there is always the other side of the coin: increase your income.

As mentioned in Chapter 3, consider dedicating an entire weekly shift, set, or tips from a certain table to your emergency fund. Alternatively, you can pick up extra shifts, another job, or find a side hustle in a different industry. In fact, all your natural hustling skills make you an excellent candidate for starting a business, and the flexibility of the industry is also great for budding entrepreneurs. Think about the classic story of the actress moving to Hollywood and waiting tables to make ends meet. It's often a great pairing. The industry can support you while you take time to build and follow your dreams, whether it's to start a business, become an artist, or retire comfortably.

You Are Not a Lending Institution

In addition to figuring out how to cut your discretionary spending, here's another tough lesson you may have to learn, just as I did: Just because you have the money doesn't mean you should lend it out, especially when you're trying to save for your emergency fund. However, as SIPs, this can get complicated.

One of the challenges with earning cash and working in the industry is that most people who know you also know you make cash, and due to the access to quick money, they may see you as someone to whom they can go for loans. This may also include your coworkers. They know that you don't have the nine-to-five systems of forced savings or automatic deductions, and they may assume you will have a harder time coming up with a reason to say no. Further, if you talk about having a great shift or large amounts of savings with people who do not understand the purpose behind it, they may also try to come to you for loans or gifts of money. It's important not to sacrifice your goals or emergency funds for the emergencies of others. Your emergency fund is not extra money. It needs to be there for you.

As a personal policy, I don't lend people money, and in pursuing the goal of becoming financially free, I aim never to have to borrow money from friends or family. If asked, my response is, "Sorry. I don't do loans, but I can help in other ways." If I have reached all of my savings goals and have a little extra for the month, I may choose to give my friend a gift of money, and maybe it's a little less than what they need, but having this boundary now helps me know that all of the progress I make will be there for me when I really need it, and I'm not just preparing for those who failed to prepare. For those in your life who are struggling financially, maybe you can't be the Oprah of your group, but you can offer many other things; you can offer to be an accountability buddy and go on a 30-day no-spend cleanse, or you can offer to sit down with your friends and help them review their spending plans.

Out of Sight, Out of Mind

Now that you have a good idea of where to find the extra funds, let's look at where to stash them once they start rolling in. The actual mechanism of saving an emergency fund can vary, but you will want to set your goal and break that goal up into small, achievable steps. Don't forget to celebrate each step of the way! One of my favorite ways to create an emergency fund is the 100-envelope challenge. This is also a great method if you prefer to deal only with cash, rather than through a bank.

1. Buy a pack of 100 envelopes and label them one to 100.
2. Shuffle the envelopes.
3. Each week, pull an envelope and put the amount written on the envelope into the envelope with cash. For example, if you pull an envelope that says 20, then you put $20 into the envelope. If you are looking to save quickly, you can up the ante and pull an envelope every day. I move the full envelopes to the back of my box.
4. Once you fill all the envelopes, you will have saved $5,050!
5. Take that money to the bank (or safe), honey!
6. Start over again!

Remember, this will be a significant chunk of change, and you'll want to keep it safe from theft or fire, so I recommend a lockable fire bag or fire resistant safe. I love physical systems, but if the envelope system seems like too much, you can also make regular deposits of all of your tips into your bank account and transfer 20 percent into your emergency fund account. I know a waitress who stops at the bank after every shift and deposits her money into her savings account.

Since we are talking about banks, I should mention that I highly recommend you keep your emergency fund in a bank where it's hard for you to spend your money yet not too hard to get to in an emergency. Better yet, put your money in a high-yield (earns interest) savings account. Regardless, the key here is to put your money somewhere else, so you don't accidentally, or purposefully, spend it.

"Fuck You" Money

Because of the association of the emergency fund with a job loss, the emergency fund has had a bit of a rebranding recently and is sometimes referred to as "fuck you" money—meaning you have enough money to cover you while you look for other employment. Google defines it as having enough money to burn all bridges. For the most part, SIPs can say, "Fuck you," to a boss, usually a couple times, and still find gainful employment in their industry, not that you should. On the other hand, nine-to-fivers dream of the day when they can finally say, "Fuck you," as they walk out the door.

As we discussed in Chapter 1, nine-to-fivers have all sorts of safety nets built into their jobs—paid sick leave, healthcare, dental plans, etc. Because of those safety nets, their emergency funds may be used differently than your emergency fund. For nine-to-fivers, they need their emergency funds to cover things like a big medical expense or to cover a job loss (especially since a lot of their safety nets and benefits are tied into keeping their job). In the nine-to-five world, finding a job takes a lot longer than in the service industry. The higher the position is, the longer the job search will be, which is why a lot of people use their emergency funds as a way to protect themselves from going into debt during a job search. The standard advice is to cover six months. Freelancers who are specialized and who work on projects are often told they should have nine to 12 months in their emergency funds.

SIPs usually have it a little easier in the job search category; we can easily land a new gig in a couple weeks, depending on where we live and the time of year. Therefore, the emergency fund for a SIP in the context of covering a job loss can be less, perhaps only three months of expenses (which is what I recommend starting with anyway). However, you may also want to boost it to cover some of the other employment benefits that we don't get. We will talk about health insurance in Chapter 9, but you may want to include some additional money in your emergency fund for sick leave (giving yourself some PTO) or dental work. In 2020, many SIPs faced joblessness for extended periods of time, and many were forced to switch industries to make ends meet. I'm not telling you to include a global pandemic in your planning, but if you were in the industry then and still are, my guess is you may not think three months of living expenses is enough.

> **Tip for the Tipped**
>
> *I like to keep my emergency fund for six months of my necessary expenses. In my head, I allocate three months for "oh, fuck" emergencies and three months for "fuck you" emergencies. In today's world, Murphy's law applies—anything that can go wrong will go wrong, and usually all at once.*

Unemployment Benefits Are Not a Plan

This is a good moment to talk about unemployment benefits and why unemployment benefits are not a plan. Unemployment is hard to get, complicated to get through, and not enough to live on. If you used this program during the pandemic, you may remember this fondly. The majority of what you received, if you received anything at all, was the COVID-19 booster, which is not a normal part of unemployment. As mentioned in Chapter 1, unemployment benefits are based on reported income. If you didn't claim all your tips or didn't even file taxes the previous year, then it would make unemployment impossible to rely on. Moreover, the websites and call centers feel like they are designed to be a hurdle. It's not intuitive, and if you have glitches in your application, it can take weeks to sort out.

Unemployment benefits may sound like the answer to losing a job until you are faced with trying to figure them out, and if you are lucky enough to receive benefits, there is the shock of the paltry amount you are told you can live on. An emergency fund is much easier and safer to build than trying to rely on unemployment to keep you afloat.

Fuck Up Funds

In addition to my emergency fund, I have one other savings account that has completely saved my sanity. It's similar to an emergency fund, and I call it a "fuck up fund." A "fuck up fund" is used for whenever you screw something up. It can sit in a separate bank account, or it can be money you keep in an envelope or cash—whatever works for you.

One example of using my "fuck up fund" was when I was working at an Irish pub as a waitress. It was one of those places where the owner hung out every night and was offended if you turned down shots from a patron. As a result, there were nights when I was very tipsy and very busy. I remember one night when I lost my billfold—the one with all my cash from all my tables for the whole night, including the order for the 10-top I had just taken. A wave of panic set in as soon as I realized I had lost it, a thin film of sweat appeared all over my body, and my stomach turned… Hard. I asked everyone on staff to help look for it, and after 15 minutes of no luck, I went back to the table to retake their order. I lost hundreds of dollars that night. Had I not had my $800 fuckup fund, I would have been devastated. I was certainly pissed—pissed at myself, pissed at my boss, pissed at the lucky bastard who found it and didn't turn it in. I was pissed for days, but I was not fucked. I took the money out of my "fuck up fund," thankful I had self-insured against these types of mistakes.

We've all been there, and it sucks. We've all counted out a register, billfold, tip bucket, receipts, purse, or whatever, only to realize that somewhere along the line there was a mistake and that we must bear the consequences. How pissed were you? Were you panicked? Were you mad at yourself or your decisions? Well, what if you had set aside money for these circumstances? What if you self-insured for those fuckups or mistakes? This could be built as a part of your emergency fund, or it could be done like I did with my "fuck up fund" and create it as a separate fund to draw from whenever you do something stupid. This "fuck up fund" would also come in handy if:

- You get a speeding ticket on the way to work.
- You show up late, and your boss sends you home.
- You scratched the car of a valet guest.

Don't get mad and make things worse; instead, know that these things happen to everyone, and the most important thing is how you react to these situations. Covering one of your small fuck ups will likely go a lot further than involving your manager in the only mistake you've had in six months. If you have prepared for the fuck ups, then you can react appropriately.

The "fuck up fund" was created out of my own circumstances, but it works for me, and you can call it whatever you want. If you don't feel like you need a "fuck up fund" in addition to an emergency fund, that is totally fair. Again, this is all about creating systems that work for you. Create your own additional savings accounts for anything else you need to safeguard against what you feel falls outside of the framework and rules you set up for your emergency fund. I wanted my emergency fund to sit there and be there for the big things, so I knew I needed to create something separate for the smaller things.

The Rebuild

Once your emergency fund (and any other safety type fund) is built, make a list (write it down) of all the acceptable emergencies that allow you to draw from it, and completely forget about it. My emergency list includes medical deductibles and expenses, home emergency repairs, job loss, and urgent trips to see family or friends. My "fuck up fund" also has rules, one of them being it cannot be used twice for the same fuck up.

If you end up using some of the fund for emergencies, plan to replenish it in the same way you built it. Decide how long you need to build it back up, and be aggressive—the sooner the better. The goal is for this money to be there, in full, at all times. I cannot tell you the amount of peace of mind it brings me. This account changed everything for me. It changed how I let people treat me, and it changed my entire perspective. The changes that resulted from those things changed my life. This emergency fund is the piece of your financial puzzle that is directly related to both choice and freedom. It's the bridge between Current You and Future You. It's the one account that is there for both versions of you. Creating and sticking to a budget and saving for your emergency fund are the two hardest elements of setting up and maintaining your plan for financial freedom. Everything else that we will cover, including investing and paying down debt, will become automatic parts of your budget. Just know, if you get this far, the hardest parts will be behind you.

> ### *Financial Freedom Road Map Steps*
>
> *Take these mindful action steps to create your emergency fund, so you can continue moving yourself closer to financial freedom!*
>
> - Create a goal amount for your emergency fund, and make a list of all the emergencies you can tap it for. Break your goal into monthly or weekly amounts.
> - Open a separate savings account just for your emergency fund (bonus points if you find a high-yield savings account that pays interest).
> - Allocate 20 percent from every shift to your emergency fund until it is fully funded.
> - Decide if you also want to set up a "fuck up fund" or any other long-term savings accounts.

— Chapter Seven —

Who Ordered the Credit Topped With Debt?

Debt erases freedom more surely than anything else.
Merryn Somerset Webb

When most people think about personal finance, the first two things they think about are debt and credit. I've left them out until now because both are huge sources of shame and judgment. Rather than focusing on past mistakes or choices, this book is about Future You, not Past You, which is why we focus mainly on budgeting, saving, and investing. That being said, we need to know the basics of what debt and credit are and how to incorporate them into our journeys to financial freedom. In this chapter, we will break down the concepts of debt and credit, how best to use them, and how to clean up or reestablish credit in tandem with paying down debt.

Debt

First and foremost, let's get one thing clear: you may *have* some debt, but you are not *in* debt, and you are not your debt. Debt is not somewhere; it is merely something—something you hold—and you can hold a lot of things at once. Life does not pause because of debt. Debt does not prevent you from budgeting, saving, or investing; it doesn't prevent you from going *anywhere*. So, what does it mean to have debt? Having debt simply means your lifestyle (your choices) or circumstances (what life has thrown at you) were bigger than what you had planned or saved for. That's it.

While debt is a tool to be avoided at almost all costs, it is never something to be ashamed of. Shame is not welcome at our personal finance party. We live in a society that has normalized debt and celebrated the decisions that put many people in debt. Think about how many times you hear, "Congratulations on the new house. You look amazing in that outfit! So happy you got a new car. Congrats on getting into your first-choice college." It's important for us to clarify that not all debt is equal. In the world of personal finance, most see mortgage debt as good, high-interest credit card debt as bad, and student loans as somewhere in the middle.

Credit

Credit is a system of borrowing money and paying it back at agreed upon terms. A credit score is a rating, given by a credit agency, that is based on how that company rates your use of credit. There are a few companies that offer credit ratings (the big three being Experian, TransUnion, and Equifax), but the most common credit score range is 300 to 850. Credit products, such as loans or cards, virtually always come with interest rates. The rates you are assigned are based on *your* credit score; not everyone gets the same interest rates. With a credit score of 500, you may see rates of 14 percent on a car loan application, whereas a score of 780 could get you an interest rate of two percent, a difference of 12 percent, compounded! That can mean a big difference in the monthly cost of your car payment.

At its core, debt is a result of credit, and how much credit you can access is a direct result of how you manage debt. Most people have some experience with debt and credit, and for a lot of people, it doesn't always go well the first or even the second time. Good credit is not something to stress over, but it can be the cherry on top of your financial sundae. Regardless of your debt and credit past, Future You will want good credit.

A Predatory System

In Chapters 1 and 2, we explored systemic issues and our locus of control (our beliefs about how much we control the events and the environments of our lives). When it comes to finances, some things are just out of your control, such as extra costs related to a serious injury or illness. Being diagnosed with cancer or some other serious medical issue will all but guarantee you end up with medical debt.

So, we need to accept that medical debt is something we have to live with and manage, that mortgage debt is mostly good, and student loans are something to be very leery of. While we cannot change much of the debt and credit system ourselves, you do have a choice with most of your purchases, and that is where you will need to focus your energy. We will dive into some changes you can make shortly, but first, let's gain some wisdom and discuss exactly why credit products are, in general, a predatory system.

The Allure

Home buying is still one of the two biggest ways most Americans accumulate wealth, and most people who buy homes do so with traditional lending. As we just discussed, mortgage debt is mostly good; getting a mortgage can allow you to purchase a home years, if not decades, earlier than if you had to save up for a house in cash. The downside of mortgage debt, however, is that the banks that preapprove you for loans might not be taking all of your life expenses into account when they determine how much mortgage you can "afford." They won't be there when things get tight, so make sure you do your own math and have a solid grasp on your numbers before getting into a mortgage.

While credit is typically required if you want to buy a home, neither home buying nor credit is essential to financial freedom. The further away we get from "mostly good debt" like a mortgage, the more predatory credit becomes. Many people have been lured into signing up for new credit cards or loan products because of the sign-up bonus, cash back options, no-interest periods, or other perks. The reason these companies can afford to offer those perks is because they know they will make more off you in interest than they ever will have given you "for free" in perks. If you have any credit card debt, and you are serious about pursuing financial freedom, then just say no to opening multiple credit cards. It's very common for people who struggle with debt to get into a cycle of paying down debt and then racking it up again.

Interest Rates

The main reason lending can become predatory is because of the interest. Interest is the extra amount you pay to borrow money, and it's what makes debt so dangerous. Here's an example. Let's say you take out a credit card with a $1,000 limit and an 18 percent APR (annual percentage rate). You go out and buy a $1,000 iPhone or put a down payment on a vacation. After some quick math, you tell yourself that 18 percent of $1,000 is $180, so the total is actually $1,180. Are you wrong? Sort of. Confused? So are most people. It all comes down to the magic or evil of compound interest.

Compounding interest magic works hard for you when you invest but gets evil quickly when you have interest bearing debt. The problem is that compounding interest is interest that accrues on top of any interest you already have. If you don't pay in full each month, this grows rapidly. Compound interest is very difficult to understand. It's not just you; for some reason exponential growth isn't something our brains can grasp easily. Albert Einstein once said the following about compound interest: "He who understands it, earns it; he who doesn't, pays for it."

> *Example: Let's do some hypothetical math on your $1,000 cell phone. Let's also assume there are 30 days in the month. You get your first bill and pay the minimum, $20 or two percent. The next bill is $980 plus $14.60 interest, and your new balance is $994.60 with only a little over $5 of your $20 going to the actual bill. On the next bill, you get charged interest on the previous balance, including the unpaid interest. If you pay the minimum payment of two percent, it will take you over seven years and $862.22 in interest to pay it off. So, your $1,000 phone ends up costing you $1,862.22.*

If you are someone who has paid down a portion of or even all of your debt, I tip my hat to you and say congratu-fucking-lations! That shit is hard work, and it weighs on you. Our capitalist society would love nothing more than to see all of us in low "manageable" (*eyeroll*) amounts of debt. Even the savviest of spenders can find themselves racking up debt in the blink of an eye. If debt had been modeled for you in your upbringing as it was for me, the debt mountain can often be a much harder hill to climb. Debt is the antithesis of freedom (reread the quote at the beginning of the chapter).

Understanding Your Debt

At one point on my journey, I had tens of thousands of dollars in high-interest credit card debt, and after defaulting on much of it, I discovered my credit was in the low 400s. Between the age of 19 and 20 years old, I had taken out over a dozen credit cards and maxed them out while trying to take college classes and renovating the house I had bought (more debt). I then proceeded to fall behind on all my payments and eventually became so overwhelmed that I stopped paying them all together. I started dealing with creditors regularly.

Once I couldn't get access to traditional credit, I fell prey to the more predatory lending services. I remember going to Rent-A-Center and signing up for weekly payments on a television and couch after a big move. When I think about how much that couch ended up costing me because of interest, I want to crawl in a hole and hide, but not as badly as how much I wanted to crawl in a hole when I learned the library can hit your credit report, which I learned after failing to return many books on CD. I also learned that medical bills from other countries can affect your credit report. I truly have tested the limits of the credit system.

That being said, once I decided to get serious about cleaning up my credit, it didn't take nearly as long as I thought. First and foremost, to get out of debt and improve your credit, you need a two-part plan: clean up and reestablish. Spoiler alert: No, you cannot use your emergency fund—not even the "fuck up" portion—to pay down your debt.

Cleaning Up

The clean-up portion of improving your credit typically consists of three things: running your credit report, determining what you don't have to pay, and figuring out how to pay what you owe.

Running Your Credit Report

For my own credit cleanup, I started by running a copy of my credit report. Your credit report will consist of your credit history, credit inquiries, and public records. Next, I made a list of all the things I needed to clean up—any accounts that had open balances. If you notice any items on your report that don't look familiar, this could be a sign of identity theft or fraud, and you will need to contact the company that holds the account for more information, as well as contact the credit agency to dispute the account. You can run a free copy every year from annualcreditreport.com.

Determining What You Don't Have to Pay

The next thing I did was determine if there were debts listed that I didn't have to pay. I took a look at the purchase/debt incurring dates for the bigger ticket items and older items. Then I did my homework. Creditors and collection agencies can only legally collect on your debts for a certain period of time (which varies state to state). My suggestion? Never pay a creditor for a debt that is past its statute of limitations. It's important to remember you might not even be paying your original debtor. You might be paying some company who bought your debt because they believed their spammy tactics would somehow convince you that your old T.J. Maxx purchases were more important than your current rent. These people are not to be trusted, nor are they entitled to your money if it's past the timeframe of your state's statute. If your debt is timebound, you cannot be sued for payment after that date has passed. This also means you cannot have your wages garnished after that date. That said, not paying the debt doesn't make it magically disappear. It can still affect your credit score and your ability to get a mortgage.

Paying What You Owe

After pulling my credit report and checking to see what I needed to start paying on, my next decision was figuring out how much I could pay toward the debt. For smaller items that were recent, I bit the bullet and made calls to pay them off. That served as a token of my commitment and got me motivated. When we talk about our three-category budget or the 50-30-20 rule, I mentioned that 20 percent of your budget is going to savings, investing, and debt, but how you break up that 20 percent can vary. In Chapter 5, I encouraged you to pay Future You no less than 10 Percent. As long as you have something directed toward an emergency fund and retirement, then the rest of that 20 percent can go to paying down debt. If your debt bothers you, it could also be advantageous to throw the extras from bigger tip nights or extra shifts toward your debt.

Climbing Out of Debt

There are four main avenues for dealing with debt:

1. **Ostrich:** It is exactly what it sounds like: ignoring your debt or mostly ignoring it by sticking your head in the sand and hoping for the best. Maybe it's not opening your bills, or maybe like me, you move out of the state and change your phone number and your hair color when creditors get to be too much. This is one way of dealing with things, but I hardly recommend it. I will tell you that after years of answering my phone anonymously with, "Hello," and responding to creditors by saying, "No. She is not here," I now love answering my phone with, "This is Barbara."
2. **Debt Management:** This approach is when you pay off the debt you have accumulated. I like this strategy best. This method involves you working directly with your creditors or working with a nonprofit credit counseling agency. If you are in ostrich mode, I highly suggest you move into debt management mode, and stay there, so you can also avoid the next two avenues for dealing with debt.
3. **Debt Settlement:** Here, you pay a company to negotiate settlement or relief with your creditors, sometimes as favorably as 40 cents to every dollar. This arrangement includes you paying back a majority of your debt along with a management fee. It's also important to note that debt settlement will show up as a ding on your credit report, just like bankruptcy. Debt settlement agencies can be predatory, so I suggest avoiding this unless other avenues have already been explored.
4. **Bankruptcy:** Chapter 7 is the most common, and fastest, type of bankruptcy. This wipes out many types of

debt. There is also Chapter 13, which is more of a debt restructure and payment plan which can allow you to keep your assets. Bankruptcy is no easy solution, and it comes with a host of its own issues. *Talk to an attorney if you are considering any bankruptcy options.*

If you aren't like I was (very committed to the ostrich method), you may already be in the process of making regular payments on all your debt. If you feel good about it, make sure those line items are in your budget, so you can ensure you continue making payments. Make it easy and mindless by setting up automatic payments (which, for some debt, may have a reduced interest rate as an incentive) and trust that time (plus occasionally checking in) will get you there eventually. It's not sexy, but it works, as long as you don't continue to accumulate additional debt.

If you are in ostrich mode, or if you fall off the wagon, start fresh and make the commitment. Meanwhile, make sure to direct some energy to the savings and investing portion of your plan because that stuff is positive and exciting, and it's where the magic of financial freedom comes from. You may be surprised at this idea because many personal finance gurus advocate paying down debt fully before saving and investing, but I really encourage a hybrid approach. Saving and investing also take a while to heat up, so those habit muscles are just as important to develop as paying down debt. No one gets to financial freedom simply by having no debt. It's important to have a mindset of growth, and most people don't have that when they are solely focused on debt. Paying off debt is a milestone to be celebrated but also one to push past. Before you can celebrate, though, let's decide how you will tackle your debt.

Payoff Strategies

Wondering which debt strategy is fastest? Considering taking a new approach to debt and hoping to optimize the process? The truth is the best tactic is the one you will stick to.

There are a handful of popular methods, which I will outline below. If one calls to you, start there.

Debt Snowball

This method is when you list all your debts from smallest to largest. You then devote extra money each month to paying off the smallest debt first, and you make only minimum monthly payments on the other debts. When the first balance is settled, you move on to the next smallest. Behavioral psychologists have found paying off the lowest balance debts first leads to the fastest "wins," which leaves you reenergized and more likely to stick to a payoff plan. Because of this, the snowball method is often touted as the best, even though it doesn't make the most financial sense.

Debt Avalanche

Logically, paying off your highest interest rate debts first makes sense as those cost you the most financially. The debt avalanche does just that. You pay extra money toward the debt with the highest interest rate, you move on to the debt with the next highest interest rate, and so on. Again, you do this while making only the minimum monthly payments on other debts. This method is sometimes hailed as the best because, financially, it costs the least amount of money to pay off the debt.

Debt Lasso

This method encourages you to consolidate your debt onto a single low-interest card or into a personal loan and throw everything you have to that one source of debt. This method combines two other strategies: balance transfer and consolidation. The balance transfer portion can get you a reduced rate, even if only for a short period, and the consolidation strategy brings everything together, which can help you focus.

Creditors

Working through your cleanup plan can take a while, and depending on your chosen strategy, you may end up having a run-in or two with a bill collector. Missed payments or late payments have happened to almost everyone. If you are overwhelmed with debt management and getting regular calls from creditors, let's pause first, take a deep breath, and acknowledge it's hard, and it sucks. I know what that is like, and it can take a toll. Second, try to remember that creditors are people, too, people who have their own money problems and likely have been on the receiving end of those calls as well. If you are dealing with creditors and levy or garnishment orders, I strongly recommend you look up the FDCPA, the Fair Debt Collection Practice Act, which outlines what is and isn't allowed by creditors. Once you know the rules in your state, you can be more confident in dealing with these phone calls or letters.

Anytime a creditor called, I would tell them I needed them to mail all correspondence regarding the alleged debt, and that once I received it, I would verify it and call them back. If they called too many times, I'd ask them for their address and tell them I was sending them a cease-and-desist letter. I remember feeling as though it gave me control, even when I couldn't make payments.

Why You Shouldn't Use Your Emergency Fund

Garnishment orders, levees, and creditors can be complicated and scary, but at the end of the day, it's just paper and people trying to get their hands on your money. Your job in this situation is to protect yourself first, while slowly and steadily paying down your debt. As discussed in Chapters 5 and 6—emergency funds and paying yourself first—you and your emergency fund come before the IRS, T-Mobile, or the nice folks down at Kansas City Asset Recovery Specialists. Your emergency fund is only for you and for real emergencies—debt is only a situation.

Your emergency fund is there to prevent you from going further into debt. It's tempting because it seems more logical to pay down interest bearing debt with money that is on hand—and mathematically there is some truth to that—but behaviorally, this is how the debt cycle gets repeated again and again. To get out of the debt cycle, you need to keep the emergency fund to prevent your debt from getting bigger and pay down your debt as quickly as you can while maintaining your emergency fund.

Credit (Re)establishment

Once I established my debt paydown strategy, I moved on to my credit reestablishment plan. For me, that meant signing up for a secured credit card with a limit of $300. That means I paid the company $300, and they used that $300 as a security deposit, which, in turn, gave me a credit card with a limit of $300. I used that card for small everyday purchases, and I paid it off every two weeks. After a few months of positive payments and positive use, my score improved, and I was able to start applying and getting approved for a traditional unsecured card.

You may be saying, "Credit is how I got into this debt mess in the first place. Damn that whole system to hell!" I get it, but here's the thing: Every day you are working and buying things, you are part of the ultimate "system" of capitalism, and shirking the parts that require more practice and self-control only serves to punish you. A better goal is to play the system to the best of your ability, and to do that you need to be in the credit system. You may need time, but when you are ready, paying off your balances in full every month and keeping a good score is the best way to "damn the man."

It's important to remember that maintaining a good(ish) credit score is largely a free endeavor. Working toward a good score is mostly making your payments on time, having a few cards with good reporting history, and low debt to available credit ratios.

> **Tip for the Tipped**
>
> To help you boost your score, keep these tips in mind:
> - Never close your oldest cards (unless they have a membership fee).
> - Keep zero or low balances, so your ratio of debt to available credit stays high.
> - Occasionally use your cards—once a month is fine (so companies don't close them due to inactivity).
> - Common credit myths you should know:
>   - Your score does not improve by keeping a monthly balance.
>   - Credit card companies will not close your card for paying your balance off in full every month. The bonus is that paying in full each month is how you avoid paying any interest at all!

As a bit of a side note, if you are unable to be a part of the credit system, either because you know yourself and know you cannot manage access to debt (which is totally cool; know thyself) or because of identity theft, documentation issues, bankruptcy, etc., there are a lot of alternative resources to traditional credit. "Buy now, pay later" is making a big entrance into our financial lives; we see it with Airbnb and with PayPal. We see companies getting into the credit game, some with interest and some just as an added perk to the product or consumer experience so as to encourage spending. While this may be seen as an alternative to traditional financing and potentially a way, in the future, to rebuild your credit, it should be noted that the effect of "buy now, pay later" reduces the tension in purchasing decisions. We need that tension in order to think critically about the purchase and whether we really need or value it or if we just want it.

Getting out of debt and improving your credit score are important to overall financial wellness and vital to financial freedom. However, it's important to remember that it should be only a portion of your overall plan. A good credit score can help you with the home buying process or renting, but your emergency fund, your budget, your savings, and your investing are far more important than your credit score, so if this one sits on the back burner for a while, that is totally fine.

> ### *Financial Freedom Road Map Steps*
>
> *Take these mindful action steps to pay off debt and improve your credit score, so you can continue moving yourself closer to financial freedom!*
>
> - Run a copy of your credit report, and save a PDF or hard copy of it where you can easily access it.
> - Set an annual recurring reminder in your calendar to run your credit report.
> - Review your report, and look for debts that need to be paid or ones that need to be disputed.
> - For debts to be paid, create a list of all debts, the totals, and a schedule for how much and how long you can take to pay them off. Then set up monthly automated payments.
> - Adopt some mantras to keep you from accumulating debt. Examples include:
>   - *I don't use credit cards unless I can pay off the card in full every month.*
>   - *I don't finance things.*
>   - *I don't open store cards.*
>   - *I don't buy what I can't afford today.*

— Chapter Eight —

Keep Your Drinks Close and Your Investments Closer

*When large sums of money are concerned,
it is advisable to trust nobody.*
Agatha Christie

Investing is vital to financial freedom. I know… Investing can also seem really complicated and overwhelming. You know what else can seem complicated and overwhelming to many? Wine. You can get way into wine. You can learn about the tannins, the grapes, the region, and the distillation process. You can talk about the barrels, the body, the mouth feel, the notes, and the age. There are whole books, courses, and degrees you can earn on wine.

Wine and investing are very similar in that way. You can read endless books, take courses, and earn degrees for investing. You can talk about individual stocks, futures, margins, dividends, growth versus value—you could dive deep and allow it to get complicated. However, and this point is important, in the same way that you don't need to dive deep into wine for you to enjoy it or for you to have a successful wine experience, you also don't need to blow tons of money and countless hours of your time diving headfirst into the intricacies of investing in order to have success and build wealth. In this chapter, we will cover some basics, just enough to get you in and get you earning—all the good taste minus the snobbery.

I promise to keep things simple, high level, and moving quickly. We'll discuss compound interest (from the magical side), why cash loses value immediately, why investing is necessary for financial freedom, what your options are, and how to get started investing immediately.

Invest, Invest, Invest

There are two major reasons people "in the know" encourage investing. The first is compound interest. As discussed in Chapter 7, compound interest means money is growing exponentially. With debt, interest works against us; with investing, it works for us. Because it's so hard for our brains to understand compound interest, especially when it's working against us, we can easily fall into a constant debt cycle.

Benjamin Franklin described it perfectly when he said, "Money makes money. And the money that money makes, makes money." Still not clear? Here is what we need to understand about compound interest when it comes to us:

1. Interest we pay is very bad—worse than we can imagine.
2. Interest we earn is very good—better than we can imagine.

The second reason people in the know encourage investing is because cash is designed to lose value. The word inflation has an extremely negative connotation, because it means your money gets you less stuff as stuff gets more expensive. But, did you know there is a reason for inflation? Inflation is a tool—an actual function and feature in our economy—to prevent the wealthy from hoarding all their money in vaults and taking a Scrooge McDuck swan dive into their swimming pools of gold each morning. The wealthy know that with this feature in place, their money loses value when it's sitting idle. They need to send it out into the world, so it can keep its value and (they hope) earn more (and this process stimulates the economy in return).

Because your cash is losing value every day, you cannot save your way to financial freedom. Even in a high-yield savings account, you will not earn enough to offset inflation. You also cannot earn your way to financial freedom. How much you make in a shift, in a month, or in a year is not a metric you can use to determine your financial position. So, how do you build wealth, and how do you get to financial freedom? Yup! You guessed it—investing. Wealth comes from investing; freedom comes from investing.

Dipping Your Toe Into Investing

Truth be told, investing is a really simple concept that has been made very complicated over the last 50 to 100 years. But if your eyes start to glaze over when you read the words "stocks" or "bonds," then not only are you normal, but you are also responding exactly how the financial services industry wants you to respond, so they can swoop in and say, "There, there. This stuff is complicated, and we are experty experts. We will do this for you, so you can get back to life, and we will only take a small percentage for ourselves." (*RED FLAG, RED FLAG, RED FLAG!*)

But, they're not wrong. It can feel complicated, until you look at it from a new perspective, one you can relate to. In reality, it's not just the financial industry that has become so specialized and complex; it's our industry, too. Just think about it. Do you ever have a guest who is simply blown away by your abilities? They may say, "How do you do that? How do you know that?" Every day in the service industry, we see new innovators and the bar is raised (pun intended). Think about old timey bars where they just had one or two liquors to choose from. Not today! A bartender will make dozens of different cocktails on an average night, using dozens of liquors and mixers.

You're an innovator, too! Every time you create a new cocktail, a new complex pole move, or a new point of service, you raise the bar and make your industry that much more complicated and specialized. It's the same in the financial services industry. Those employees also innovate and come up with their own cocktails to set themselves apart from the pack, only their cocktails are a mix of companies, assets, products, or accounts, which we'll talk about more soon. Understanding that the financial service industry is similar to our own and expanded like our own will help us better connect to the professionals and the products, so when we get into it, we're going to use some familiar industry terminology to learn about investing.

First, just know you'll need to get comfortable being new in this space. It's just like when you were new to the service industry. Now that you've been there a while, you can probably spot a newbie a mile away. *They are unsure of the words on the menu or don't know the services you offer. They ask for things such as a vodka and Coke, a well-done steak, or for your phone number.* In every industry, there are things you need to learn to make the most of your time there. Since we plan on using and having money for the rest of our lives, we should get comfortable with knowing we need to be open to learning about the specifics of money and the financial industry.

Investing at Its Core

So, what, exactly, is investing? Maybe a better way to answer this question is to start by reviewing what investing is not. Investing is not buying lottery tickets. Investing is not getting sucked into a multilevel marketing "business" (MLM) where you have to buy inventory of beauty, "health", fashion, or home products and pressure your friends, family, and community into purchasing them. Investing is not gambling because with gambling, you don't own anything; you need to own things for it to be an investment.

Investing is also not speculating; speculating is more guessing and hoping. For example, speculating would be opening a restaurant when you know the majority of restaurants fail, and you've never even been a GM.

Investing and speculating are often confused; both involve risk, and both involve making choices, but the difference is the probability of success versus failure. We have 100 years of history on the stock market, so we can make educated predictions about the overall market, and we know, based on that history, there is a high probability of success in investing in the overall stock market long-term. On the other hand, picking the stocks of individual companies is much riskier, so on the scale of speculation versus investing, buying shares of individual companies would lean more toward speculating since there is a stronger likelihood you will lose your investment. The same would be said for picking individual crypto currencies. There are a lot of options, and the probability of you picking the right one—the one that will shoot up in value—is highly unlikely.

The word "investment" is thrown around a lot these days, so let's talk about how to react to incoming "opportunities." Always remember two things:

1. Think critically (and skeptically) about the potential investments that cross your path. If it's new, it's not investing—it is speculation and gambling.
2. As SIPs, we have a variable income which means that all the investing we do should be more stable than what others may invest in.

For our purposes, investing is when you own things, when you buy and hold those things (meaning you don't sell them), and when those things have a high probability of increasing in value or can generate income for you while you own it. "Buy and hold" is one of the most trusted strategies available. Buy things, own them, and sell them only when you need to.

Take a Seat and Have a Drink

Do you ever get a guest who is so overwhelmed by the menu? You ask questions but can't really gauge what they want or what their preferences are, and trying to walk them through some of the options has them nearly running for the door. That is probably how you feel as an investor right now.

Think of what you usually do for that guest. If you are like me, you serve them something that will work for almost everyone, something easy on the pallet, one of your go-tos. It's usually mid-priced and is good enough to get them to come back. You don't scare them off with something overly complicated. That's what we're going to do in this chapter—sit you down and serve you up something tasty.

I can tell that you are already salivating, wanting to know what investment I would recommend for you, so you can get in the game, have some fun, and start earning that compound interest. You likely don't know what your risk tolerance is, but you know you want enough risk to make big gains yet have enough safety, so you can ride out volatility. You want something you can just set and forget and let it work its magic while you sleep.

Before we get into the nitty-gritty details of investment, we first need to have you understand the framework and layers for how investing works. To do so, let's use something we know all too well as a vehicle for understanding the complex world of investing: the bar. As I outline investing, think of it as a trip to your favorite spot.

Two Investors Walk Into a Bar...

Let's start at the bar. The bar is where everything happens. In the world of investing, you would start off at the institution which is also called a brokerage house. This is a company that sells you financial services, accounts, and products. Instead of going to Patsy's Pubs or Shooters Sports Bar where you buy your drinks, you will go to places or websites like Vanguard, Fidelity, or Charles Schwab to buy your investments.

Once you get to the bar (brokerage), you'll want to order a drink. The bartender doesn't simply pour cocktails into your mouth and call it a day. No! Drinks need to be served in something. The glassware is equivalent to the various accounts the brokerage can set up for you which will hold your investments. They both hold the thing you are buying. The account types vary just as much as the types of glassware a restaurant uses.

Where the bar uses vessels such as a pint or martini glass, the brokerage uses vessels (i.e., accounts) such as a 401(k) or a Roth IRA. The containers are owned by the bar and brokerage, even though the liquid assets they hold (booze and money) are owned by you.

Next are the cocktails themselves. The cocktails are what the bar sells to us, whereas investment funds are what the brokerage sells. We look at the menu of cocktails (list of funds), check the price, and place our order (buy or transact). The drink itself can be anywhere from a neat pour (a single liquor) to a complex blend of liquors and mixers. The liquors are the exciting and risky elements, and the mixer is what smooths it out and makes it a little safer. In the world of investing, your investment fund can also be made up of a number of things, like stocks (liquor—riskier) and bonds (mixer—safer).

So, to compare and recap:

In drinking, we have:

- The bar which controls the glassware.
- The glassware which holds the cocktail.
- The cocktail which is a mixture of liquor and mixer.
- The liquor and mixer which is what we own.

In investing, we have:

- The brokerage (e.g., Vanguard) which controls the accounts (e.g., Roth IRA, solo 401(k))
- The accounts which hold the investment funds (e.g., index funds, ETFs).
- The investment funds which is a mixture of stocks (e.g., Apple, Tesla, Amazon) and bonds (e.g., treasury bonds).
- The stocks and bonds which are what we own.

From Happy Hour to All Hours

Now that you understand the layers of investing, let's dig into those layers and clarify some of the terms we used above. We will start with brokerages. Brokerages offer different portfolios or accounts with different levels of service, just as different bars offer a different array of wines, cocktails, or beers with varying levels of service. There are a few types of brokerages you should be aware of:

- **Full-Service Brokerages:** These will be your high-end, country club or hotel bars—think wineries or private tasting rooms. You walk in to a temperature-controlled room and know you will have a fully curated experience. You also know you will be spitting wine into a metal bucket, and the fees will be incredibly high. If you make oodles of money or have a huge inheritance, then this could be a good option for you.

    Examples: Merrill Lynch, Morgan Stanley, Edward Jones, J.P. Morgan

- **Discount Brokerages:** These are my favorites, the places where your everyday millionaire and mom-and-pop investors set up their accounts and choose their investments; it's like stopping in at your favorite local pub for happy hour to enjoy a couple of cold drinks after a long day. These brokerages offer low-fee funds and have good enough interfaces where you can make your selections, but they are not so overly sophisticated that you get lost on the homepage.

    Examples: Vanguard[1], Fidelity, Schwab, E*TRADE

---

[1] I personally use Vanguard because they are a co-op and member owned, but as long as you find a discount brokerage that offers low-fee index funds, then getting started now is much more important than spending months in analysis, only to realize they offer pretty much the same stuff.

- **Investment Apps or Online Advisors (Robo-Advisors):** Robo-advisors are online advisors connected to a brokerage house and app. The "advice" is pushed out by an algorithm, which is where the "Robo" (robot) comes in. The newer companies and apps sometimes encourage an active or day trading approach or even offer loans which can lead to gambling behavior and statistically lower returns. I caution against the majority of these because some offer advisors push products, and some even sell your investment data. Can you imagine going to the 24-hour hipster bar next door to your house and finding out the bartender was selling a list of everything you drink? That would be incredibly creepy.

    Examples: Robinhood, Webull, Wealthfront, Betterment

Whichever path you choose, I encourage you to simply get started. Choose a brokerage, go to the website, and create a login and a password. You are one step closer to investing!

Choosing the Right Glass

Sticking with the analogy of cocktails as investments, the glassware represents the different types of accounts out there that can hold your investments, and each comes with different features and rules.

- **Traditional IRA:** We will use the pint glass to describe the IRA, which stands for individual retirement account. The pint glass is not the best glass out there, but it's definitely the most versatile. The pint glass can fit any drink into it, it's partly a shaker, and it can also hold straws in a pinch. I liken the pint glass to the IRA (otherwise known as the traditional IRA, not a Roth) because the traditional IRA is the most widely available vehicle for retirement savings. The IRA can be opened by anyone earning taxable income living in the U.S., including all SIPs. It's not the best, but sometimes you have to use what you can, and it's much better than nothing!

> **Tip for the Tipped**
>
> *You do not need to involve your employer or use your paycheck to invest in an IRA. You set up the account yourself and transfer money from your bank account. If you are primarily a cash earner, be sure you are claiming more income than what you are contributing to your investment accounts.*

- **Roth IRA:** A Roth IRA is like a Collins glass, also known as a highball glass. It's the best glass for a cocktail or mixed drink with the perfect amount of space for ice, liquor, and a mixer. The Roth IRA is arguably the best account type out there because your money grows tax free, and you can pull it out tax free once you get to retirement age. It also has the added bonus of allowing you to pull out the money you've put in as contributions before retirement (59 ½ years of age) if you ever find yourself in a true emergency.

> **Tip for the Tipped**
>
> *Unlike a traditional IRA, a Roth IRA has an income limit, which is why it's not as big as the pint glass. With the Roth, you can claim up to $129,000 in annual income (as of 2022) and still contribute to this account. As with the traditional IRA, the Roth IRA also has a contribution cap. If you want to contribute more than $6,000 (as of 2022) to your investment accounts, then you will need to complement this account with another account, which we will discuss next.*

- **Taxable Brokerage Account:** This is the martini glass of accounts. This account is not a designated retirement account, but if you need another account to build up your investments, the brokerage account is always an option. The martini glass has the largest surface space of all the glassware, relative to its contents, and you have full access to all the liquor, so you need to be careful when drinking them. If used properly, a martini is a damn good time and the perfect drink; if used improperly, you pay the price—the same goes with the taxable brokerage account. Here are three important notes about the brokerage account:

  1. First, let's be clear on the lingo. A brokerage firm is where all the accounts live, so technically *any* account offered at a brokerage firm is a brokerage account, but for some reason, as a society, when we talk about a brokerage account, we only talk about the taxable (ordinary) brokerage account—not an IRA, Roth IRA, or 401(k).
  2. As SIPs, this is also the perfect vehicle for someone who needs to have access to their funds at all times. Unlike a retirement account which prevents you from accessing those funds until you are 59 ½, years old, a brokerage account is a great way to have money on hand.
  3. You do need to pay extra attention to this account because it carries annual tax consequences based on the moves you make, such as if you earn income or pull money out.

- **401(k):** The champagne flute is what we will use to represent 401(k)s. The 401(k) is typically provided (i.e., set up, not contributed to) by your employer. This is very fancy for tipped workers because most don't have this luxury, which is why we are choosing the bougie champagne flute for this example. A 401(k), which is named after a tax code, is a retirement account that is held by your employer or, occasionally, the state. It's similar to an IRA in that there are Roth and traditional options.

> **Tip for the Tipped**
>
> *If you bounce around from employer to employer, it will likely be easier to set up your own IRAs, as transferring 401(k) accounts out of your employer's name can be super annoying.*

- **Solo 401(k):** The snifter glass is a super specific glass with the purpose of capturing and retaining the aroma of its contents. It also has virtually no stem, which means it's meant to be handled—your hand touching the glass and warming the contents is part of the experience—and you are part of crafting the cocktail experience. If you are a contract or freelance worker, with no W-2s or tax deducted paychecks, then you are technically both the employee and the employer. This means you have access to account types that are also super specific, ones that recognize your role as the curator of your employment experience as an employer.

    As a true entrepreneur, you have the responsibility of tracking all your work-related expenses in addition to your income, as well as all the headaches of keeping receipts and sorting them out at tax time with your CPA. The upside is, being self-employed means you have access to a solo 401(k). If you have an EIN (if you don't, you can get one from the IRS very quickly), this account is awesome. You can shovel heaps of money into it, which is great if you are making a very good income and know you might only be doing this for a few years (looking at you, dancers). You and your employer (which is also you) can contribute up to $61,000 total each year, as of 2022.

- **Whole Life Insurance or Other Annuities**: This type of account is like the shot glass. As with a shot, it is not the liquor inside that makes this such a dangerous choice; it is the glass and how it functions. Think about it—with the majority of people who walk in and say, "I need a shot," you know it's likely the last thing they actually need. On top of that, think back to when you've done shots; out of 100 times, likely only two of those times were actually a good idea. Whole life insurance and annuities are the same in that out of every 100 people who are sold them, only two of those people were an appropriate fit. Further, those two people just happen to already be extremely wealthy. We will get into insurance in the next chapter, but suffice it to say, these insurance products that also claim to be investments are often pushed onto the wrong people because they come with a high commission.

Mastering Our Selections

Now, let's get into our drinks or our funds—the stuff we own! There are a few different types of funds, but the most popular funds are mutual funds, index funds (mutual funds that copy indices), and ETFs (exchange-traded funds). These are groupings or baskets of investments; funds are a collection of securities, just as a cocktail is a collection of its ingredients.

- Selecting **actively managed mutual funds** with a full-service brokerage firm is similar to going into that really high-end, fine dining restaurant and ordering the most expensive bottle of wine because it's supposed to be the best. The wine list (aka, the investment list) is either a dozen pages and too complicated to read, or there is no menu, and the server will simply make selections as they see fit. This is what you are paying a premium for—the curation, the latest hype, the points of service, and the status of a specific fund manager who is on a hot streak.

> **Side Note**
>
> Statistically, no fund manager has ever beat the overall market for the long-term, so unless you are dying to pay for this experience (and once you are in it's hard to get out), then I would skip this option.

- Choosing **index funds** (mutual funds that copy an index—essentially just a popular list of companies or securities) with an online discount brokerage firm is similar to going into your neighborhood bar and getting the house red. The bar has six wines in total—three red, two whites, and a sparkling. They have a $12 glass of dry red and a $20 glass of dry red; both are good, so you go with the $12 red. It's a solid night out, and you didn't have to do the dishes. Investing at an online discount brokerage firm may not have the latest tech or a fancy hedge fund manager selection, the same way your neighborhood bar and grill won't have a wine sommelier, but because of their low fee, more of your money goes into the investment, and they can build you some serious wealth and help get you to financial freedom. Most index funds are passively managed and mirror other popular and successful indices.
- Picking your own **ETFs** inside of your online discount brokerage is similar to going to the 24-hour diner and ordering a can of champagne with a bendy straw. You can get a lot of options at any hour you want, and there is usually a picture with a very accurate description of what you will get. An ETF is similar in that they are usually a low-fee fund, you can buy or sell even when the market is closed, and they are very transparent with what they are holding. Just as you can purchase that can of champagne instead of the whole bottle, with ETFs, you can also purchase fractional shares.

Example: VOO is the name of a popular Vanguard ETF that buys shares of 500 of the best companies.

The Recipe Calls For...

We've discussed where to invest, what kinds of accounts you can use to invest, and the different types of funds you can select as investments. Now, we need to discuss what the hell is inside those funds—what are these "investments"? There are many types of investments, but we will talk specifically about what investments you can buy in the stock market.

Just as bars are similar to investment companies, bar managers are similar to fund managers. When bar managers create their cocktail list and select spirits, they look for cocktails with high-quality ingredients that pair well to create the perfect balance—one that has the right mix of risk or reward and safety or stability. Many great bars stick with the classics—they are tried, tested, and always deliver.

Many advisors use a classic as well, especially when it comes to the balance of how much risk and safety is included in their funds. Here's a rule of thumb that always delivers:

- Take 110 and subtract your age; the number you are left with should represent the percentage of your investments that should be invested in something safe and stable; this is your safety percentage.
- Now take 100 and deduct that safety percentage. The number you are left with should represent the percentage of your investments that should represent risk.

Example: If you are 35, your stability/risk ratio would be 110-35=75 (75 percent risk, 25 percent safety). This would be your risk profile or, as it is sometimes referred to, your asset allocation.

Both "risk profile" and "asset allocation" are super jargony terms that simply mean how much of the alcohol (growth/

risk) versus mixer (safety) you want in your investment cocktail. Remember, with safety, there isn't much growth, and with risk, there isn't much protection, which is why this balance is important.

In summary, to choose one thing from each of the layers to set up your investing strategy, it can look like this:

1. **Select your brokerage (bar).** Example: Vanguard.
2. **Select your account type (glassware).** Example: Roth IRA.
3. **Select your securities/funds (cocktail).** Example: 70 percent Vanguard total stock market index fund (this fund is the risk/reward, or the alcohol) *and* 30 percent Vanguard total bond market index fund (this fund is the stability, or mixer).

The above would give you a solid experience. It would be like the vodka, soda approach—a little boring, but it does the heavy lifting, especially when you have other goals and things to focus on.

Stocks and Bonds

When most people talk about funds and securities, they are mostly talking about a mix of stocks and bonds. Stocks and bonds, for simplicity, are certificates that are sold to raise money for starting a new company, for expanding an existing company, or even for raising money for cities. Stocks are shares or a fractional percentage of a publicly traded company. When you buy shares, you are a small, but partial, owner of the company. Bonds are shares of a loan.

> *Example: Your city needs new roads, so they offer bonds. The buyers of the bonds provide the money for the roads, and when the roads are done, the city pays you (one of the buyers) back with the taxes provided by the taxpayers (with interest).*

Stocks are typically seen as riskier but also more rewarding, whereas bonds are seen as safer but don't deliver high or fast growth.

The stock market itself is not one place, but a general term for the collective places where you pool, buy, sell, and trade. When you hear, "The markets are up today," that usually refers to one of the indices that follows a group of companies and, more specifically, refers to the Dow Jones index which follows the stock share prices of the 30 biggest companies.

Other Investments—Real Estate

That was a lot of information, and if you want to hit pause and go pour yourself a drink, do it! I get it! But, also take a minute to appreciate the fact that you just took a minicourse on investing, and you now know more about investing than probably 90 percent of people.

I love investing in the market. I like that the U.S. government has an organization called the SEC, and they keep an extra eye on the publicly traded companies to make sure they are operating above board, which adds another layer of protection to your investments. I like that the market has a low bar for entry, meaning that transaction costs can be low, and you can get started investing with very little money; in fact, you can start investing today with as little as $10. Outside of the market, there are a few other places you can invest, such as real estate.

Ever heard the phrase, "Your home is your best investment"? How about the phrase, "You can never go wrong with real estate; they aren't making more land..."? A lot of people have a lot to say about real estate. I love it, but I also hate it. I have had success, and I've had failures. Who doesn't love a thrill ride like that?

I've been mostly successful with real estate. In fact, the other industry I have the most experience in outside of hospitality is real estate (renovations, development, design, property management, investing, etc.). You can invest in real estate by buying a property and renting it out to earn cash, or you can buy a personal residence and build equity as you pay down the loan or make improvements, which you typically only recapture if you sell. However, I don't want to talk about real estate investing here. Instead, I want to briefly discuss why making the decision to own a home should be done differently for those who are in the service or hospitality industries.

To Buy or Rent? That Is the Question.

The first thing to remember is that there is no shame in renting. In fact, renting can be a great strategy for wealth building.

Let's say that 25 percent of your monthly income (what you take home after taxes and deductions, or your net income, as financey folks say) is $500. A typical rule of thumb is to spend no more than 25 percent of your income on your home. As a renter, you can spend $480 a month on rent and $20 on renters' insurance, and you're done. As a homeowner, if you can afford $500 a month, there are other expenses outside of the mortgage you need to consider as part of that equation. You need to consider the cost of maintenance and repairs, property taxes, and homeowners insurance, to name a few.

If you don't have a solid emergency fund, then a portion of your monthly home cost would need to go to building up a reserve for things such as roof repairs, appliance repairs, a new hot water tank, or your furnace. How about taxes? Is there a cost for sewer, trash, or recycling? By the time you add up the additional costs, owning a home can be substantially more expensive than renting.

A mortgage payment of $500 with all the extras mentioned above can add up to or average at $800 a month. Instead, if you rented that $500 apartment and invested the difference, there would be a very compelling argument that you could build more wealth by renting and investing the difference, rather than in buying a permanent residence. However, if you are someone who knows you will be staying in the area for more than six years, you have an emergency fund, and you can house hack by living with roommates, then I very much encourage buying your primary residence. In fact, house hacking and home ownership, if your portion of the mortgage is less than 25 percent of your income, can be a great catalyst to building wealth. In a way, it's forced savings. You can build equity in the home and still have room in your budget to save and invest.

Still not sure which one is right for you? Your past behavior and tendencies can help predict whether it would make more sense to buy or rent. Consider these factors:

1. **Time:** Do you plan on being in the same city for six years or more? It often doesn't make sense financially to buy a house, pay the closing costs and broker fees, and sell it in three years.
2. **Flexibility:** I have lived in more than five different major cities in the last fifteen years! It is one of the top perks in our industry—people need help, so there will always be a job somewhere. If you enjoy the flexibility of this industry, don't let society tell you that you aren't a grown up or you aren't successful simply because you don't own a home. That is bullshit. You are a grownup when you make the best decision for your life.

> *Example: I once took a bartending job at an airport, convinced there would be the occasional patron who had just been dumped. In my head, they would walk in with this great trip all planned out, an extra ticket in hand, no one to go with, and tell me everything while I served them drinks. Eventually, I would tell the patron, "I'm adventurous, super fun, and always carry an extra pair of underwear and a travel toothbrush. I'll go with you!" Appallingly, in the 12 months I worked at the airport, I was never offered a free getaway or a buddy pass. I'm still shocked. I'm also shocked that I'm shocked or that I ever thought that in the first place.*

For some people, like me for many years, owning a home won't align with your lifestyle. For others, it's a great fit. Are you, for example, a single, savvy hustler with extremely strong ties to your current area? Maybe the idea of buying a three-bedroom and renting it out to two other SIPs, using their rent to help you pay down the mortgage—thereby increasing your equity—is your idea of a good time and a good investment. If that is the case, far be it from me to dissuade you as there could be a big payday if you decide to sell later. However, if you are more of a "I got drunk and applied for a job on a resort in Cabo and accidentally got hired for the winter season" kind of person or even someone who likes to keep their job prospects open, then renting may be for you, and that is perfectly okay. Either is totally fine.

Why You Should Invest

Let's recap. We started talking about investing in Chapter 1 when we explored how most SIP employers don't provide 401(k)s and how most SIPs don't prepare anywhere near adequately for retirement. Investing serves many purposes, the largest being providing income for your retirement or early retirement (due to disability or desire). Even if that is the main goal, you are not limited to investing only in retirement accounts, and that's great, too—either way you go, investing in either retirement or nonretirement accounts has many benefits (besides funding your retirement):

- Investing helps you avoid having money erode due to inflation.
- Investing helps you grow your money (money making money while you sleep).
- Investing helps you create more options (taking a year off of work or scaling back and working part-time).

Investing and using compound interest to make your money work for you are vital pieces to building wealth and getting closer to financial freedom, and the sooner you start investing, the sooner compound interest can begin to work for you. The two biggest contributors to wealth building are the amount of time in the market and your contributions; both are things you can control and make the most of if you start today.

> ### *Financial Freedom Road Map Steps*
>
> *Take these mindful action steps to start investing today (and every day), so you can continue moving yourself closer to financial freedom!*
>
> - Open up a Roth IRA, and link your bank account (if you claim less than $140,000 per year). If you are ineligible, open up a traditional IRA.
> - Set up automatic monthly purchases of index funds or ETFs of your choosing. I like index funds that represent the whole market for diversification.
> - Double check your work! Call the 800 number of the brokerage firm you are investing with, and ask them to walk you through purchasing the funds, and ask them to confirm it's set up properly and that the transactions have been processed.
> - If you are able to invest more than $500 a month ($6,000 is the current limit for Roth and traditional IRAs), open up a regular brokerage account and contribute anything over that $6,000 into the brokerage account. You can buy index funds for this account, too!

— Chapter Nine —

Cover Your Ass (When You Aren't Twerking)

There is no harm in hoping for the best, as long as you are prepared for the worst.
Stephen King

If you've ever worked in a club or a bar, then you've likely relied on security staff. I have counted on big beefy bouncers to escort countless drunks out who have gotten way too handsy with me, and I am forever grateful. I can't imagine how I would have otherwise escaped from a few really scary situations. They were there when I needed them but also when I didn't. We all need a little help when things get out of hand. Think of insurance like that because sometimes life steps outside of what we can control; insurance is there to cover your ass when you need it most.

Insurance is also one of the most infuriating topics in personal finance. It's overly complicated, it's always changing, and it feels like a "gotcha" is on the other side of trying to use any of your policies. I wish I could say there is a way to automate a simplified insurance strategy that will cover all your needs, but unfortunately, as with all things insurance related, you need to be a diligent and educated consumer to make sure your ass is truly covered.

In this chapter, we will review four of the main types of insurance: health insurance, life insurance, property and casualty (covers auto, home, and rental), and disability insurance. We will discuss what products to avoid, what are must haves, and what are the best practices for being a well-informed consumer.

Health Insurance

I am always stupefied that I went over a decade without any insurance coverage of any kind, especially healthcare. Many of those years were before the Affordable Care Act and the marketplace, when you could be denied a policy for a preexisting condition. I'm glad a marketplace exists, and that preexisting coverage is now a requirement, but the system is far from good. Statistically, "they" say you are only one serious illness away from bankruptcy, which is what makes health insurance so important, but it's also what makes it so infuriating. To keep my sanity, I have managed to do a little bit of a mental reframing. These are the things I tell myself:

- Health insurance is just a cost of life, like taxes. Shake your fist, stomp your feet, curse the world, but then accept it, find a way to pay for it, and move on. (Bonus points if you write to your government.)
- Health insurance can protect you from bankruptcy when major health issues arise. Don't think of it as a policy for providing coverage of all your healthcare costs but rather as a layer of protection from everything else you've worked so hard for being taken from you by medical debt.

Why You Need It

As professionals who deal with the general public on a constant basis, we are at a higher risk of germ exposure and of catching colds and viruses simply by the very nature of our jobs. Having to constantly touch things other people touch, especially things that have been near people's mouths means we have to be more diligent about protecting our health than others. That includes making sure we are covered for basic healthcare services.

When we discussed being excluded from traditional employer-provided benefits, health insurance was one of the biggest benefits on that list. Big companies have their HR department research different health insurance plans and choose options based on things that are (or they believe are) important to their staff. Typically, nine-to-fivers are offered two different plans with two very different deductibles, and they are able to make their decisions without much effort or research.

Tips and Tricks

You, on the other hand, someone who is not trained to understand how to decipher different policies, need to wade through dozens of options to find a policy that fits your needs. There's no doubt it's overwhelming. However, like everything, take it one step at a time. Start by visiting www.healthcare.gov to peruse plans in the marketplace. Make sure to look at the following terms, and understand how each would impact you:

1. **Deductible:** What you have to pay out of pocket before your insurance kicks in.
2. **Coinsurance:** The portion of the cost you are responsible for after insurance kicks in.

    Example: If your bill is $200, your coinsurance may be 20 percent, which means you pay $40, and the insurance company pays $160.

3. **Maximum Out-of-Pocket:** The limit of what you have to pay within a plan year for covered expenses.
4. **In-Network/Out-of-Network:** Whether a doctor, hospital, or provider accepts your health insurance plan.

> **Side Note**
>
> *Some facilities can be in-network, while some of the service providers providing care within that facility are out-of-network. Tricky, tricky.*

One time, I used a Groupon to get a dental cleaning after many years of no professional cleanings. I went to a place that didn't require insurance, and man, did they try to upsell me—more than that, they shamed the shit out of me. They told me all the things that were wrong and used scare tactics. I told them, "I have enough money for a cleaning today. Everything else will have to wait." I walked out irritated with them, but I was also proud I advocated for myself. Sometimes you have to make trade-offs, and sometimes you need to remind yourself that you and your doctor should be making plans surrounding your healthcare together in a holistic way, and that includes discussing your financial life.

While we cannot control much about the healthcare system, there are a few ways to potentially reduce your premiums:

1. **Smoking** (or other substances) increases the cost of monthly healthcare premiums, as well as the lifetime spend on healthcare-related costs. Cutting back or quitting altogether can reduce premiums, in addition to providing other health-related benefits.
2. **Take care of your overall health.** This reduces visits and can allow you to opt for a higher deductible plan which would reduce your monthly spend. This means getting good sleep, resting when your body cues you to do so, drinking water, and eating healthy.
3. **Don't wait too long to seek care.** Waiting until things get too bad can mean more money in many ways. In an emergency, you aren't going to call around to make sure that the hospital is in-network. Further, emergency and urgency room visits are much more expensive than a visit to your doctor.

4. **Preventative care saves money.** Get your annual physical and your annual dental cleaning. Preventative services also aid in catching serious health issues early on which can cut down on treatment time and overall expenses.
5. **Health is wealth.** Some insurance companies give you premium credit or even cash back for things like having and using a gym membership or completing an online nutrition course.

Life Insurance

Financial freedom means you are not burdening anyone else with your financial obligations which extends beyond healthcare to end-of-life costs as well. This means making sure your debts do not pass on to your loved ones, that your dependents will be cared for, and that end-of-life costs, such as your funeral and burial, will be covered.

Life insurance is intended to provide money to your dependents or beneficiaries following your death to cover the gap of your missing income, or to help your loved ones reimburse themselves for the costs of your end-of-life expenses and settling your estate. The last thing you want is for your loved ones having to start a GoFundMe for your funeral expenses and stressing that they won't get enough donations while they also try to grieve your loss; even worse is them putting themselves in debt to pay for your services.

> *Example: Assume you need at least $20,000 to sort out the end-of-life arrangements, including $8,000 for the funeral (which is the average cost), $3,000 for settling your estate, and another $9,000 to pay any final bills or monthly expenses while the estate gets settled (medical bills, mortgage, car payments, utilities, storage units, etc.). It's expensive to die, and no one escapes death.*

On a quick side note, an "estate" is what we leave behind after we die. Everyone has an estate, even if you don't own a home or consider yourself a wealthy person. An estate can consist of your checking and savings accounts, your investment accounts, cash, furniture, cars, clothing, jewelry, pets, and all your other belongings. Your life is not a grab bag for those around you to pilfer from and rummage through after you die. Every state has laws about how your assets must be dealt with.

Most states require estates to be dealt with in a process called probate. This is the court's way of protecting your rightful beneficiaries, while still allowing for all parties to make their claims (creditors, estranged family, your delusional aunt who believes the card she received with "all my love" translates to "all your possessions"). Some things can bypass probate if they are held jointly or have a designated beneficiary (retirement accounts), but this stuff is complicated, and since financial freedom means you are planning on having assets, it is best to get comfortable with the idea that you need to do a little Googling on how your state's probate laws work. Plan on working with an attorney to create a will. Creating a will should not take more than a few hours and a few hundred dollars if your estate is straightforward, and it will save your family or friends a lot of grief and fighting if all your wishes are written down and held with an officer of the court.

With your estate planning and an adequate life insurance policy in place, you can be assured your family will have an easier time managing the fallout after you're gone.

Choosing the Right Kind of Life Insurance

What type of insurance is right for you? Good question! Let's look at the options. There are two types of life insurance: term and permanent.

1. **Term Life Insurance:** This type of insurance covers you for a set period of time. A term policy often makes the most sense because once you have a fully funded emer-

gency fund, and your investment accounts add up to the amount of your coverage, then you can be considered self-insured, and you can drop the policy.

It may be helpful to think of this as a temporary component of financial freedom that you need while you build your savings and investments. Life insurance is, for most, meant as income replacement for your spouse and your dependents. Once you no longer have dependents, and no one is relying on your income, then you no longer need insurance (as long as your savings can cover your end-of-life costs).

Example: If you don't have dependents (kids, a spouse you support, or aging parents), then you don't need to replace your income, and a small policy would make a lot of sense. A 20-year term life insurance policy of $50,000 for someone in their 30s can cost as little as $10 a month. If you have dependents, then you will need to calculate how much income you need to replace to have someone care for your dependents in the event of your passing. For instance, if you have a 10-year-old, you would want a policy that would cover the time until they turn 18 years of age. You could start with a 10-year term policy that includes covering the loss of your income ($50,000 a year of income would mean that you would want a $500,000 policy). A 10-year term life insurance policy for $500,000 for someone in their 30s can cost less than $25 a month.

Tip for the Tipped

Choose the less expensive, less complicated policy. Just get started!

---

2. **Whole Life Insurance:** Also known as permanent insurance, this type of insurance offers coverage for your

whole life until you die. We touched on this in Chapter 8. Other names for permanent policies to look out for are "universal life insurance," "traditional whole," "income for life," and "annuities." These products claim to be part investment, part insurance and work by having you pay a premium until a set date (typically when you turn 65 years old), at which point they are paid in full, and you can draw them down or have them set aside to be paid out in the event of your death. Life insurance is for risk management—if you have an extremely high net worth and a lot of money, this insurance could make sense for you. However, the average insurance product investment return is around 1.5 percent, whereas the market averages around eight percent, which means your money is more likely to return much more if you invest in the stock market rather than a whole life insurance product. For your average person, this product is a scam and is pushed in a high-pressure sales situation because people who sell permanent life insurance make big commissions.

Property and Casualty Insurance

Aside from the big two—health insurance and life insurance—both property and casualty insurance and disability insurance provide additional coverage for all your insurance needs. Whether or not you need this type of coverage varies based on your personal circumstances.

Homeowners' or renters' insurance are other important policies you should be putting in place to protect where you live, what you own, and the financial life you are building.

These policies can also carry personal liability protections that extend beyond just your home or your possessions. For example, if someone tripped and fell on the steps of your home and sued you, your policy could provide coverage for you in that situation. Some policies will even cover your wedding jewelry while you are wearing it—for example, if you lose it on vacation while swimming in the ocean.

As with all insurance, read the fine print closely. Consider car insurance as an example. The majority of states require car insurance, so if you drive a car, you likely already hold casualty insurance. If you were to rent a car, many assume that the service renting the car, the credit card you are using to book the car, or even your standard car insurance has all the necessary coverage should an accident occur. That is not necessarily the case. Check your specific policies and lenders to understand exactly what coverage you have.

Disability Insurance

As a tipped employee, you move around a lot, and you are on your feet for long hours at a time. This can take a toll on your body, especially if you aren't great about general fitness or are someone who often works until burnout. Given this, long-term disability insurance may be an option you want to explore.

Full disclosure, I've never had a disability policy. The reason? Most policy claims only pay out for three years, not permanently. I just don't want to pay monthly for a policy that only covers me for something that specific. If I had a disability that prevented me from working for only three years, then I would drastically cut my spending and lifestyle and make my one-year emergency fund stretch for three. In my head, I'd rather save that money and keep stocking my emergency fund. I can't imagine a time in my career when I would have purchased this type of policy for myself, but it's important you know it is an option, so you can make an informed decision.

If you got through this chapter and are thinking, *Man, that is a lot of insurance doom and gloom*, you're right. There are a lot of corporations that make money off reminding people that it could all be gone in an instant. While that is fear mongering and the epitome of capitalism, the fact of the matter is all it takes is one accident for people to be severely impacted without these policies in place.

I consider the majority of these policies to be mandatory—a necessary evil—for financial freedom. You cannot change your financial life overnight, so you need to layer these in over time.

> ### *Financial Freedom Road Map Steps*
>
> *Take these mindful action steps to cover your ass as you continue moving yourself closer to financial freedom!*
>
> - Get quotes for life insurance, open a term policy, and set up monthly automatic payments.
> - Get quotes for health insurance, review your options, enroll in a plan, and set up monthly automatic payments.
> - Create a will, and let your loved ones know where they can access your end-of-life and estate planning documents (I recommend a local, lower cost attorney).
> - Save all your documents to a safe location. If you prefer digital, you can use a cloud storage account, Google Drive, external hard drive, or thumb drive that is password protected. Create separate folders, and label and date your documents. If you prefer old school, get a fireproof document safe. Whichever you use, make sure someone else, such as your attorney, knows where they are and that they have access.

— Chapter Ten —

Money on Your Mind(set)

*Whether you think you can,
or you think you can't—you're right.*
Henry Ford

We've spent the last nine chapters talking about how you earn your money, and what to do with those earnings (expected from a book about money). However, in my opinion, this chapter is the most important one of all, and it has nothing to do with spreadsheets, envelopes, or investment bankers. In this chapter, we will get a little more in depth on the fringe or philosophical as we talk about your body, how it supports your mind, and how that supports a healthy money mindset.

Your money mindset encompasses your attitudes and beliefs about money, as well as how those beliefs show up in your life. I've heard many financial experts state that "getting good" with money is 20 percent math and 80 percent mindset. Another way I've heard it is, "The money part is easy; it is the behavior part that is hard." The math and strategy part were covered in Chapters 1 through 9, with a little bit of mindset sprinkled throughout. Now, we need to dig deeper into mindset and also discuss support of the mind and body, so all the hard work you are doing for your financial future can serve you for years to come.

What is Your Money Mindset?

When I was starting out, if someone would have told me I needed to work on my money mindset, my first response probably would have been, "What the fuck are you talking about? I cannot pay my bills or book my vacation with my mind," or, "Must be *so* nice to have *so* much time that you can just think about this woo-woo shit" (*rolls eyes*). But, if someone would have told me they taught a course that could help me save more money, and by the time I left, I would feel wealthy and confident with money, I would have signed right up. Here's the thing: We all want results, but no one talks about how to get them. It turns out, results come through working on your money mindset.

As I said before, our mindset is made up of our attitudes and beliefs about money and how those attitudes show up in our life, but what does that really mean? How do we find out what our attitudes and beliefs are? How do we know if they need to be changed? If they do need to be changed, how do we go about creating that change?

> *Example: Here's a belief you may have heard: "Rich people are evil, greedy, and selfish." This belief could be subconsciously keeping you broke, so you aren't labeled one of those "selfish people" by the people you love. Maybe you don't believe this, but you know your peers and family do; as a result, you may downplay your success, so you don't get "too big" for your circle. Maybe you join the chorus of "I'm broke, so it's impossible to get ahead." This mindset could be causing you to sabotage yourself, which will get in the way of attaining your financial freedom.*

Let's start with the first question: How do we figure out what our mindset is? If our attitudes and beliefs are built on our experiences, then we need to dive into our experiences. A popular way to reference these experiences is "money stories." Everyone has a money story; you likely have many.

A money story is a pivotal memory (or collection of memories) that tells a story about how money has shown up in your past that shapes your views and behaviors around money, today. Take some time to think about your first few memories around money. Do you remember getting an allowance, wanting something you had to save for, being told there wasn't enough money for something, witnessing an argument about money, or watching someone you know celebrate a windfall? I have a few stories I can recall, mostly negative. There was the time I lost $100, which was a ton of money to my family, and I walked up and down 10 blocks for two hours looking for it. There was a vivid memory of hearing my parents argue about money. I also remember times after my mom left home when I was responsible for paying the bills at the tender age of 12 and knew we didn't have the money to cover them. I witnessed debt and reliance on credit cards as a normal part of my dad's life. Because of that, I also fell into a debt cycle early in my life.

Reviewing my money memories helped me realize I had a scarcity mindset—a mindset where I was constantly focused on my lack of resources, almost obsessively so. I would quickly spend money I earned because, deep down, I believed someone or some expense would take it. I did this subconsciously because I craved control. I encourage you to take time to explore your money memories. Here are some prompts to get you started on that journey down memory lane:

- What is your earliest money memory?
- How did you learn about money from your family?
- What was the relationship your family, peers, and neighbors had with money?
- What were things that signified money or wealth for you when you were growing up?
- What is the most positive money memory you have?

The Psychology of Money

There is a rapidly growing field dedicated to the study of money stories and of the psychological impact they have on our lives. Our relationship with money has led behavioral psychologists to create its own specialty, the psychology of money, which is the study of our behavior with money. It turns out that my scarcity mindset is real and has real consequences.

A scarcity mindset can show up in your life in several ways. One of the biggest and most detrimental ways is anxiety surrounding money. This anxiety about money manifests itself by only allowing you to focus on your current situation, and it doesn't allow you to make long-term plans or goals. Anxiety and scarcity mindsets lead to avoidance of both minor and major financial decisions. It's so pervasive, in fact, that living with a scarcity mindset can keep people from checking their account balances, which can lead to bad habits such as overspending and causing accounts to overdraft. Even worse, it's one reason why many people never save, invest, or plan for their retirement.

A scarcity mindset can also manifest in the following ways:

- Never taking risks, such as buying a home or investing
- Feeling resentful of others for what they have
- Hoarding food or other items or surrounding yourself with clutter
- Impulse spending on things you were deprived of early in life
- Feeling guilt when spending money on items that aren't completely essential
- Feeling pressured to support other family members, even if you can't afford to

However scarcity shows up for you, it's holding you back, so let's get clear on which experiences are shaping you, so you can make sure your future is not defined by your past.

Building an Abundance Mindset

Shifting to an abundance mindset is a big goal, and it will take time, but it's worth it. By looking at your money stories, you may discover memories that are contributing to your scarcity mindset, or you may also have unprocessed traumas or self-limiting beliefs. An abundance mindset can help with those as well. With an abundance mindset, you will see and believe that there is plenty of [insert anything] for you in the world. You will get to a place of knowing what enough is. As a result of knowing there is plenty of love, money, opportunities, and time, you will go out in search of those things, and you are very likely to find some of what you seek.

Some of you may be ready to scream because you know there are finite resources such as time and money, and you can't simply wish yourself a bigger bank account. In Chapter 2 you learned you can't put yourself or your job down, so you need to craft statements that are both true and positive, and you need to do the same thing with your money beliefs. An abundance mindset means figuring out where *truth* meets *possibility*. There are four strategies that, when enacted either individually or combined together, help to create the mindset you seek: charity, gratitude, identity, and mantras.

1. **Charity:** This first strategy sounds counterintuitive, but one of the best ways to build an abundance mindset is by giving to charity and those in need. Yes, by giving away your money, you will likely become better with money. Giving actually does something to your brain. Your brain thinks, *If I have enough to give to others, then I clearly have enough.* No amount is too little, but if money is too hard to part with right now, start by giving your stuff or your time. It's also important to remember that charity should be a part of your budget, so it never should come before paying yourself first.
2. **Gratitude:** Another way toward an abundance mindset is by practicing gratitude. Start by listing a few things

you are grateful for at breakfast each day. When you take time to notice and appreciate all the things you have, you train your brain to focus on what you have, not what you lack. Your brain needs to practice that because your brain's job is to keep you alive (which means continuously searching for more resources). Your brain wasn't trained to recognize the concept of "enough," so you need to actively work toward appreciating what you have and knowing what your "enough" is.

3. **Identity:** Crafting a new identity with supportive language can also help you with your money. If you use statements such as, "I'm broke," "I don't have any money," or, "I'm not good with money," you are building an identity of a broke person. Your words shape your thoughts, your thoughts shape your actions, and your actions shape your life. So, you need to begin with your words.

Instead, craft language that is both positive and true. People who study habits note that building the idea of your identity first helps to facilitate and strengthen the habits that the identity will support.

Example: If you are trying to save money, then you are a saver. Start there and adopt that identity trait; you are someone who can save. Build on that. Start using those words when you talk about yourself. You aren't broke. You simply "have a lot of obligations for your money right now." You aren't bad with money. You are "getting good with money." You don't have zero money. You are "in a wealth building stage." It's not, "Mo' money. Mo' problems." It's, "More money gives me more choices."

When you tell yourself and others you are building wealth and working on your path to financial freedom, you will reinforce the identity, you will restate your goals, and you will be much more likely to actually achieve them. Your words matter, so don't throw them away.

Start thinking about who you are with your money and who you want to be. Then, use your words, like every other resource you have, to build the life of your dreams.

4. **Mantras:** Personally, I tackle my scarcity mindset with mantras. My favorite mantra is one that should be easy for most SIPs to adopt: "Money comes easily and frequently." As someone who earns tips, money does come easily and frequently to you. I say it anytime I feel anxious about money, and I've been saying this to myself and others for over 10 years.

    I love mantras because, like identity, it's where truth meets possibility. Also, they are a free resource! Other mantras could include:

    - Money always finds me.
    - Most of my guests are generous tippers.
    - I always have enough.
    - I always figure it out.

    With these mantras, you will remind your primal brain to take a chill pill with the panic and freak outs. You've got this, and this is your way of reassuring your brain that you are not relying on a few shitty experiences from your childhood or ancestors to set the stage to sabotage you.

Mindset work is not an exact science (yet), but as with learning most things, you will build up an awareness and explore areas that resonate. No one can say what will work best for you; it's like finding what types of food or exercise work best for your body, and it takes a little trial and error.

Decision Fatigue

There are other concepts that circle around psychology that, if explored, can help us improve our minds and wallets. One is decision fatigue. Decision fatigue refers to the psychological phenomenon that as the day goes on and the more decisions we have to make, the worse those decisions get. This means after working a double, which SIPs do frequently, you are more susceptible to make poor decisions or decisions that are not in line with your goals or your values, simply because you worked that double.

This fatigue applies to your willpower and to the quality of the decisions you will make. Translation: Post work drinks, fries for dinner, and online shopping are the moments when your budget will get blown. If you reach decision fatigue, then you won't be thinking about your budget or your savings goals—you will be thinking about grabbing tacos and margaritas. You aren't saying yes to these things because you can't stick to your goals. You are making those decisions because your brain has created direct pathways to say yes to cravings that trigger the brain's reward system, especially when you are tired.

Once you've used up all your willpower (which is like a muscle and gets weak after use), and once your brain is tired, you won't care that your "eating out envelope" is empty, and you are using emergency savings to pay for dinner. Decision fatigue works in two ways, in that your decisions get worse when you are fatigued, and the more decisions you make, the worse your decisions will get—and worse decisions will always affect your wallet.

Removing Choices

You've learned a lot of different strategies in the first nine chapters that you will want to implement, and those tasks, such as budgeting and investing, will take mental energy, energy that you may not have right now. Therefore, you need to find ways to cut down on your current mental output and decision making, so you can save some of it to apply to all your new-found money plans. Saving mental energy helps you set up these systems and is vital for sticking to them.

You may be thinking to yourself that you aren't having to make that many decisions throughout the day, but in reality, it's not only complex decision making that causes decision fatigue. Remember Steve Jobs, the famous Apple CEO? He wore a black turtleneck every day, so he didn't waste any decision-making energy on selecting what to wear for the day. It's these small decisions that add up and lead to poorer decisions later in the day, decisions that will cost you real money.

Repeat After Me

Let's touch on an example of a decision you may be making that you probably aren't categorizing as a "decision": when your guest doesn't know what they want, and they want you to choose for them or make suggestions. Not only is this obnoxious, but now you are having to make a snap judgment and decision about who this person is and what would be best for them based on very little information. Do you have to do that more than once a day? Each time adds up, and they all count as separate decisions.

One way to avoid this fatigue is to give everyone the same suggestion, which is likely one of two things: either your personal favorite or a high-cost item. You may get bored saying the same thing over and over again, but you are helping to make more and better decisions for *you* later on in the day. This is, of course, not always an absolute rule. If you recommend wine to a guest who is looking for a very specific taste profile, you may not get out of helping to make those decisions, and in fact, a good recommendation can always help build on an overall satisfactory experience. This can also mean better tips. Try to get better at spotting the differences between those two scenarios, and you'll be better off.

The Power of the Pen

Another place you can avoid decision fatigue and save some mental energy is by writing everything down! Don't be that gal or guy who says to their eight-top, "Actually, I don't need a pen and paper because I've got it all up here," while pointing to your head. This rarely impresses people, and it's more likely your guests will be nervous something will be missed. Why use precious brain matter for remembering orders for others when doing so may bring you to decision fatigue? Your mental stamina is a resource, and as with all your resources, pay yourself first.

Fortune Over Fashion

It may seem crazy to copy a nutty CEO like Steve Jobs, but you are wasting precious brain capital deciding what to wear, how to do your hair, or what accessories will bring a little bit of whimsy and fun to the outfit. If simplicity is the name of your game, try buying a few of the same items, and make it your signature look. A lot of guests like returning to a place because they are comforted by familiarity and constancy. Having that signature look helps put guests at ease. It's why a lot of places have a uniform; it provides guests with a sense of safety and consistency. If your place of employment doesn't have a uniform, I highly encourage you to develop a version of your own.

Now, if you are a quantity person, and change is the spice to your life, I encourage you to narrow your focus to one item—maybe it's having a dozen different pairs of earrings or a handful of flashy shoes. If you typically work five shifts, try to put your item into an exact rotation, maybe they can coordinate with a specific day of the week.

Food Shouldn't Be Your Foe

I know people who eat the same thing for lunch every day, simply to avoid having to make that decision. However, if you are like me, a big part of the joy I experienced from serving was seeing the enjoyment guests had from their dining or drinking experience. I also get a lot of joy from experiencing new food and beverages. Something to note, though, is if you work somewhere for more than a few months, you've likely tried everything, at least everything affordable.

The average consumer spends 13 percent of their income on food and beverages, so if you are paying for food where you work, even if you get a discount, my guess is you are paying much more than that. Meal planning, shopping, schlepping, and prepping can seem like a big pain in the ass, but you should add up both the health and financial costs before continuing with the status quo. Food is mood, and a good mood earns more tips.

Caring for Your Body

As discussed in Chapter 2, this industry can be hard on the body. In choosing this industry, you are agreeing to exchanging your body for capital. You are what is known as working capital; you have to protect yourself to the same extent as you would protect a million dollars. You, yourself, and your life of work, if protected and used properly, can bring you to that million dollars. Let's look at a few bad habits you can kick to take better care of your best ass(et).

Your body is your livelihood, and, just like the horse taking steroids for the sake of one race, using excessive caffeine or uppers to get through a shift helps for the short-term, but it hurts you for the long-term. Since service industry jobs are not thought of as long-term positions, long-term thinking has a tendency to fall by the wayside, as was discussed with investing and savings. Short-term thinking is how you stay broke and sick. So yes, walking into a kitchen every half hour to eat loose French fries sounds great when you're in the middle of your shift, but you are only hurting yourself long-term. I once worked in a club where every single item on the menu was fried, even the meatballs. It's hard to seem as though you are doing "hot girl shit" when you walk into the club with your brown bag salad and ask if you can borrow a little fridge space, but once the initial moment of embarrassment is over, you can actually set an example for everyone else by saying, "I'm not spending part of what I make here tonight to pay to eat here tonight." You are not there to pay to play, and you should definitely not pay with your health. Showing those around you that you value your time, your money, and your body teaches people how they need to value you, so set the bar high.

There are also a few other body-related bad habits that SIPs tend to fall into that can negatively impact their bodies and, ultimately, their wallets. I consider them to be almost extreme sports in service and hospitality.

1. The long-distance pee challenge, or "extreme holding it," is the first. While this would be considered crazy to anyone at an office job who can stand up and walk to the bathroom anytime they feel that feeling, service people will hold it for hours as they run around, only to make it to the bathroom with barely a second to spare. If you haven't pushed your bladder to its limits, then have you really even worked in hospitality? The crazy part of this behavior is that when you break it down, you are putting everyone else's needs before your body's most basic functional requirements, and that is fucked up. By breaking this bad habit, you will make mindset shifts to put yourself before the needs of your guests, which is the way it should be.
2. Extreme dehydration is another one. Considering the amount of caffeine and alcohol consumed by tipped employees, it's no wonder most are constantly dehydrated. We are adept at navigating challenging and physically demanding days without water or food. While it sounds like something to be proud of and a way to get merit badges, I'll be the first person to warn you about the downside of dehydration with two words: kidney stones. Your kidneys need you to drink water to evenly flush out impurities in your body. When those impurities build up, they can cause stones in your body that you have to pass.

Water also makes you look younger and helps you save on moisturizer. It's basically free under eye cream. Water helps our bodies generate new cells for hair and skin. If you are a guy and you are beginning to see the signs of hair loss, then you should know that your hair actually stops growing if you aren't drinking enough water. Water will slow you down a bit because you'll need to take more bathroom breaks, and it literally makes you look younger and more attractive; as studies show, people tip attractive people more. Therefore, more water equals bigger tips.

Health *is* a moneymaking tool and though it's incredibly hard to make this a big priority in this industry, if you stay focused on rest, water, and healthy fuel, it will reap countless financial benefits along the way, all while keeping you looking your best, which even the most expensive jeans simply can't compete with.

Sleep Deprivation

Since we have discussed fatigue and health, I'd be remiss if I didn't talk about getting a good night's rest, which is very uncommon in our industry. Arianna Huffington famously wrote about how work exhaustion and fainting led to a serious injury and changed the way the media mogul thought about work and sleep. You may not be running a media empire like *The Huffington Post*, but you probably do run around a lot while you're sleep deprived. Learning lessons from successful people is how you will, at the very least, follow in some of their money footsteps. So, while it may not always be possible to avoid a double, listening to your body is actually a way to invest in yourself. Make sure that between doubles, or in preparation of one, that you get enough rest because being rested helps you make better financial decisions.

Dreaming About the Future

Speaking of sleeping, the last topic I want to cover is related to your dreams, or life goals—your "why." You don't *need* a reason to get on solid financial footing, and in fact, one of the reasons I wrote this book is because so many SIPs are still figuring things out, but I will say that sticking to goals is much easier to do if you have a "why." I'll bet you never work harder than the shifts leading up to your vacation. Why? Because you can practically feel the beach, taste the cocktails, and see the cute outfits you packed.

Financial freedom is your why, but it's more effective when it's visceral, when you can see and feel what you are working toward. Financial freedom looks different for everyone, and I encourage you to make a list of reasons you are working toward it. One of my reasons is I want to retire before I'm too old to actually enjoy it. I want to be able to say no to work or shifts I don't want to work. I want to travel to exotic locations, I want a hot tub, and I want a hammock. Those are the things that make my heart sing. In Chapter 4, regarding budgeting, you wrote out and thought about your perfect day. Pick something visual from that perfect day, and keep it in mind whenever you feel restless on your path. You can also print it out or make a vision board.

Financial Freedom Road Map Steps

Take these mindful action steps to overcome scarcity and improve your money mindset to continue moving yourself closer to financial freedom!

- Focus on building an abundance mindset—spend more time thinking about what you have and less time about what you don't (gratitude).
- Give back. Donate money, time, or belongings (charity).
- Craft your financially free identity by finding like-minded people to share your financial goals with (identity).
- Come up with a money mantra (or twelve) that feels true and is in line with your goals

(mantras)—I am responsible. I am capable. I am a saver.
- Reduce the impact of decision fatigue; try to make important financial decisions (e.g., working on your budget or investments) early in the day or on your days off.
- Build support habits. Your financial health improves when you improve other areas of health and life. Drink more water, get eight hours of sleep, listen to your body, and protect your energy.

Last Call

And just like that, you've completed a book on finance. Take a bow. You took your precious time and invested it in developing your awareness and education around your money and your future. I'm proud of you. I hope this is merely the jumping off point for your financial education. You have built an awareness around money that you never had, and you are committed to improving your financial life and working toward financial freedom.

Don't forget to continue your personal finance education. While I have not come across other personal finance books that are geared toward tipped workers, I have learned a lot from other financial experts who dig deep into the many topics we reviewed in this book. I like to think of this continued education as maintenance learning, and there are a wide variety of options you can choose from. Consider some of my favorite maintenance learning opportunities:

- **Go to www.tippedfinance.com** and check out our additional resources page. You can also reach out to

inquire about additional support, such as individual or group coaching.
- **Come back to this book.** Reread this book—new takeaways will emerge each time! Or just reread the Financial Freedom Road Map Steps at the end of each chapter. Take consistent action!
- **Podcasts:** This is my favorite medium as I walk a lot. If you are allowed to listen to something with your headphones in while you roll silverware, wait for your set, or do your side work, double win! I suggest putting on an episode of either *So Money* or *Afford Anything*. Again, you won't find it geared toward SIPs, but you will gain confidence in your own strategies and solidify your grasp on the industry language by listening to the stories and advice of others. The first 10 episodes may feel similar to listening to a foreign language, but stick with it.
- **Blogs:** If you prefer to learn while sitting in front of a computer or phone, search personal finance blogs, and you'll have plenty to choose from. Also, if you are part of a minority or other community or group, there are many specialized or niched personal finance blogs that are geared toward serving people of color, LGBTQ (like me), immigrants, womxn, former military, etc.
- **Personal Finance Books:** There is a whole section of finance books, both at the bookstore and in the library. You can absolutely buy books to build your knowledge and repertoire, but free is a great way to find authors who might be more your flavor. Plus, checking out books from the library helps you save money! Ask your library which e-reader service they belong to, and you can borrow a copy on your Kindle or e-reader, or you can get them on Audible if you prefer the listening experience. A few books that got me started on my path include *The Millionaire Next Door*, by Thomas Stanley, *Your Money or Your Life*, by Vicki Robin and Joseph Dominguez, and *The Richest Man in Babylon*, by George Samuel Clason.

- **Social Media:** Tailor your social platforms. Remove accounts that make you feel envious, inadequate, or pressured to purchase. Follow personal finance accounts that inspire and educate, such as @tippedfinance. If you are unsure how to find the content you like, start by following a few hashtags, such as #budgetingtips #personalfinance #financialfreedom #envelopesystem #503020.

Investing your money in continued education means investing in yourself. It means setting yourself up for success down the road and valuing yourself enough to commit to it. Now that you are on your path, I have three final requests of you:

- **Stay connected.** Holding yourself accountable can be tough; drop me a note and let me know how you are taking action, what spoke to you most in this book, or to share a win. Confused with something or just need a cheerleader to keep you motivated? I'd *love* to hear from you! I can be reached on Instagram or Facebook using @tippedfinance, and you can find me at www.tippedfinance.com.
- Writing and publishing this book is one of the ways I am investing in myself, just as you reading this book is one of the ways you are investing in yourself. If you got value or increased your knowledge from this book, please **leave a five-star review on Amazon**. This is the equivalent of a good tip for authors. The more reviews a book has, the greater the reach. Help me get the word out to SIPs around the country.
- **Be a leader.** You are now a knowledge leader in your community, and you also need to help others in our industry reach financial freedom. Provide your community with support, knowledge, and resources. Give this knowledge away freely and frequently. Share this book, talk about your budget, become a mentor, or start an investing or budgeting club. Community will make it easier for everyone to feel supported, and it will help to

keep you motivated and on track. Help me change the industry from the inside and start a tipped revolution!

Above all, never stop learning and investing.

~ Barbara

About the Author

Barbara Sloan is the founder of Tipped Finance. She once lived in her car, danced for dollars, and definitely did not graduate from college. She is also a personal finance expert and money coach who spent two decades working in the service industry all over the country. She now helps tipped workers achieve financial freedom as she did. She is passionate about all the amazing aspects of tipped work and passionate about all the terrible aspects of tipped work. She lives in New York City with her wife, an esteemed corporate finance executive, and together they are a couple of adorable money nerds who point out every dog they see.

Appendix 1
Road Map for Financial Freedom

Follow all the Financial Freedom Road Map Steps at the end of each chapter to achieve financial freedom.

Financial freedom means you have control over your finances and control over your choices. This could be interpreted in many ways, but to me, control over your finances means that the following are true:

1. You have a fully funded emergency fund (three to nine months of living expenses) or one that is well on its way.
2. You are consistently paying down debt and not accumulating more.
3. You have set up accounts for retirement and long-term savings goals, and you know your target numbers.
4. You are tracking your net worth (monthly, quarterly, annually).
5. You know your budget numbers and where you would cut back on spending if your financial life hit a roadblock.
6. You have identified what types of insurance you need and have put policies into place.

Control over your choices may mean:

1. You have a few ideas of what you could do if your place of employment went out of business.
2. You know that if you were ever put in an uncomfortable or unsafe position in work or in life, you have available resources to get out of those situations.
3. You have the resources (both personal financial resources and employment support) to take time off work for health and relaxation.
4. You have confidence surrounding your ability to earn and save.

Appendix 2
Additional Concepts for Financial Freedom

The 25x Rule: This guideline helps people get an idea about how much money they should set as a retirement goal. How it works: Take your average annual spending (or 12 times your average monthly spend), and multiply that number by 25.

> *Example: I spend $48,000 per year (or $4,000 per month) and therefore 25x is $1,200,000 ($48,000 x 25 = $1,200,000). This means that since my spending is $48,000 per year, then I would ideally want to aim for $1.2 million for retirement.*[1]

Don't be overwhelmed by this number. Remember, we said you aren't saving your way to financial freedom, so you aren't going to have to save $1.2 million. You will have compounding interest magic to help your money grow and double (likely a few times).

Buy-and-Hold Investment Strategy: In 2014, Fidelity did a study on the demographics of their *best* performing investors. The winner was a tie between dead people and people who forgot they had an account. The point is that buy-and-hold is the best investment strategy. There is no need to waste your time or energy being fancy or trying to pick stocks; just buy the overall market. The finance bros didn't beat the dead investors who simply stayed course. Since 1926, if you held an index of stocks for any 20-year period, your stocks went up 100 percent of the time.

---

[1] As noted in Appendix 4, $250 per month for 40 years (at 10 percent average return) will result in $1.3 million.

Rule of 72: This rule helps you to do fast math when trying to guess what your net worth will be in the future. Think of it as an estimate to see when your money will double. If you take your estimated rate of return (e.g., 10 percent is the average long-term overall stock market return) and divide that into 72, then you get the number of years it will take for your investments to double.

> *Example: Let's say I have $50,000 in the stock market in my IRA, and I'm estimating a 10 percent return. I would take 72 divided by 10 and get 7.2 years. So, in 7.2 years my $50,000 should be close to $100,000 if the market makes good on average returns.*

The 4% Withdrawal Rule. *The Trinity Study* is a trusted financial paper used to discuss safe withdrawal rates for retirees (i.e., how much money you can take out each year so you don't run out). The paper states you can take out four percent of your investments every year, and you most likely won't run out of money. This is another helpful shorthand when trying to figure out roughly how much you can take from your investments each year.

> *Example: If you have $500,000 in your retirement account at 50 years old, using the 4% rule assumes you can safely take out four percent—$20,000 per year—and you likely won't run out of money.*

Grow the Gap: Earn more, spend less, and invest the difference. This is the concept behind building wealth.

Appendix 3
Be Your Own Sharon

Sharon is our hero from human resources. She looks out for employees and makes sure they set up and use their benefits. She also helps automate the process, so it happens without costing employees any mental energy. We need to put on our "Sharon hat" and set up our own benefits.

Retirement: Set up your IRA account and a brokerage account, link your bank account, and set up recurring monthly transactions. This is one of the most impactful roles of HR—helping you to fund your retirement.

Health Insurance: Shop the marketplace for affordable plans during open enrollment, and understand what your deductible, coinsurance, and maximum out-of-pocket expenses will be. Set your premiums as automatic monthly payments. Be an educated consumer; know what is in-network and out-of-network.

PTO and Vacation: PTO and vacation make for happier and healthier humans and employees. Open a separate checking account and label it "PTO." Deposit the equivalent of five to 10 days' worth of pay. If you average $100 a shift, put 10 days, or $1,000, into the account. Throughout the year, make sure you take days as you need them, and transfer the funds to your regular checking account, so you feel as though you got a paid day off. Keep any unused "days off" in the account. Once you get down to one or two days, start the process of saving up for the next round of five to 10 days. You could also make this a January savings goal, when you "fund" your PTO account for the year.

Annual Review: In the service industry, we often miss out on the annual review, the time employees are told they are doing a great job, how appreciative their employer is of all their hard work, and potential ways they can improve. To do this for yourself, first set a recurring annual calendar reminder. When the day arrives, go ahead and give yourself a personal assessment. Feel free to write it out. Include a recap of your year, how you have grown, and examples of where you went above and beyond. Take this one step further and see if your manager wants to do this with you, and while you are there, see if there is an opportunity for negotiating better shifts, a higher hourly wage, or free food. Make sure it's a two-sided conversation by asking how you can better help your management team.

Compliance: HR helps to make sure your employer stays compliant with local, state, and federal labor laws. Educate yourself on your rights, and know what an employer can and cannot ask of you in your state.

Appendix 4
Compound Calculator

The SEC provides a free compound calculator:

https://www.investor.gov/financial-tools-calculators/calculators/compound-interest-calculator

When you plug your numbers into a compound calculator, you have to guess what your return average (gains) will be. The stock market has returned an average of 10 percent per year over the past 50 years, though there were many years when the market had little or no gains. A more conservative long-term average would be six to eight percent, but 10 percent is the actual average.

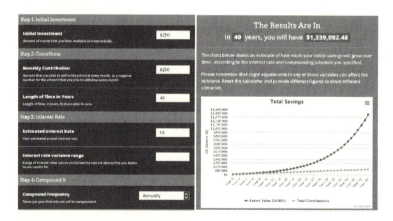

As you can see, investing $250 a month for 40 years would result in over $1.3 million. Think about the years you could shave off of your working life if you added more to your IRA and brokerage account every month.

Appendix 5
Monthly Budget Tracker

Month: January					
50% Essential		**30% Lifestyle**		**20% Future**	
Mortgage/Rent	$1,200	Dining Out	$300	Retirement	$400
Utilities	$140	Travel	$100	Emergency Funds	$200
Groceries	$320	Entertainment	$180	Debt Paydown	$180
Phone	$65	Subscriptions	$50	Additional Investment	$75
Insurance	$310	Beauty	$90		
		Clothing	$50		
		Car	$380		
Total Needs	$2,035	Total Wants	$1,150	Total Saved	$855
% of Spend	50.37%		28.47%		21.16%
TOTAL	$4,040				

*If *all* dollars are included, then the total should equal your monthly income.

Budget tip: Focus on reducing your big three types of expenses to find more balance in your budget and lifestyle: housing, transportation, and food.

Appendix 6
How to Calculate Your Net Worth

On the next page is an example of a monthly net worth tracker to use to calculate your net worth. Remember, your net worth is your assets minus your liabilities. Net worth is calculated in three steps, which you can repeat on a monthly, quarterly, and annual basis:

1. Add up your assets.
2. Add up your liabilities.
3. Subtract your liabilities from your assets.

Tracking your net worth is the equivalent of taking your financial temperature. Are things moving in the right direction? In the following example, you can see this person's net worth improved from January to February as they increased their asset accounts and paid down their liabilities.

APPENDIX

Month	January	February	March
Assets			
Checking Account(s)	$1,315	$1,420	
Savings Account(s)	$2,800	$2,800	
IRA	$2,200	$2,400	
Brokerage Account	$800	$1,000	
Cash	$280	$350	
Other	$0	$0	
Home Value	$210,000	$210,000	
Total Assets	$217,395	$217,970	
Liabilities			
Credit Card 1	$1,900	$1,800	
Credit Card 2	$0	$0	
Personal Loan	$0	$0	
Car Loan	$8,900	$8,800	
Student Loan	$27,000	$26,900	
Mortgage	$180,000	$179,800	
Other	$0	$0	
Total Liabilities	$217,800	$217,300	
NET WORTH	-$405	$670	
Change	$0	$1,075	

Made in the USA
Columbia, SC
18 November 2022